Horse Latitudes
Chris Wilson

Horse Latitudes
Chris Wilson

Sorika

First published in Great Britain in 2013 by Sorika

Edited by Thomas Rees & Gareth McConnell
Designed and typeset by Helios Capdevila
Printed by GGP Media GmbH, Pößneck (Germany)

Thank you to John Gladdy, Richard Greer, Ben Ingham,
Zoe Kealey, William Ogden, Andy Salt and Erika Winstone.

All rights reserved. No part of this publication may be
reproduced in any form or by any means without the permission
of the publishers or the author.

All text and images copyright © Chris Wilson & Sorika 2013
except lyrics from Iggy Pop, *Pumpin' for Jill* (page 51), Iggy Pop,
The Passenger (page 53), Lou Reed, *Kill Your Sons* (page 78) and
Iggy Pop, *Sister Midnight* (page 104).

ISBN 978-0-9575573-0-7

Edition of 1000 copies

Cover image:
St Genet, 2008

ABOUT THE AUTHOR

Chris Wilson was born in 1961 in Newcastle-upon-Tyne, and grew up in Dar es Salaam, East Africa. He moved with his parents to California in 1971. After many years of living in the streets and prisons of the USA he was extradited to the UK in 1998. Since becoming drug and crime free in 2001 he has studied at the Chelsea College of Art and Design, where he was awarded a First with Distinction. His work has been shown in galleries in London and the South East of England. He lives in London with his girlfriend and two dogs, and divides his working life between his job as a project worker with the homeless and various creative endeavours. *Horse Latitudes* is his first book.

The first time I saw Ñaki he was in the back of a California Department of Correction bus loading up at LA County Jail for transport to Eloy Federal Penitentiary in Arizona. My little crew was the last to board and the bus was full of border brothers and sureños who'd finished their terms and were bound for deportation. Other than me he was the only white boy on the bus, but he was sitting proud like a shot caller laughing and joking in Spanish with the tattooed La Raza. I remember thinking who the fuck is that as we headed out towards Barstow and Vegas in our paper suits and shackles.

Ignacio was a six foot two Basque from San Sebastián in Spain with slicked back blonde hair and sky blue eyes, he didn't speak a word of English other than "fuck you" and "got a cigarette gabacho?" We ended up getting celled together in Eloy and as we walked through the door we both headed for the bottom bunk and sat staring at each other. I was big but he was bigger and for five minutes in the silence we did that little OK Corral showdown 'til he smiled, patted the bunk and said "andale nosotros dormir aqui", which roughly translated means: "OK, we can both sleep here". I threw my stuff on top.

Ñaki was my buddy, my celly, my road dog, my homey and all those embarrassing words they use in the pen that filter out onto the street. We shared our canteen, our tobacco, the stuff we won playing spades and pinochle against the Vietnamese and Cubans and Mexicans, he played the back in our handball games in the yard, he liked playing hard ball with a pair of boxers wrapped round his fist, I preferred the soft ball 'cos that's what I learned with and the hard ball beat the shit out of your hand. Eloy was in the middle of the Arizona desert, not that I ever saw much of it, it's funny how you can spend so much time in a place and not know where the fuck you are, but if you listened you could hear it, the desert I mean, you could hear it each morning at 5.30 when the hoofs of the Indian ponies flew by or in the yipping of the coyotes as they fought over the prison scraps. The desert has a beautiful silence but you can only hear it if you are truly alive, and in prison that's what I was, truly alive, or so I believed.

Ñaki said he was going to die, he was sure of it. He was waiting to be deported back to Spain where he'd fled six years before after robbing 80,000 from the farm house his father owned in the hills, 80,000 of ETA money taken from a bank job in Madrid. He said they'd probably shoot him at the airport or else get him in jail where he was heading for outstanding warrants, he and his girl had come up with a way out of San Sebastián and like all good junkies they didn't think too much of the consequences, just broke in took the cash and flew to Bogotá where they spent it in six months of speedballs and insanity. When the money ran out she started turning tricks and he was recruited to smuggle station wagons with the panelling stuffed full of coke from Tijuana into San Ysidro and that's how he'd ended up in my cell. It didn't add up but I wasn't complaining. Four years of state time instead of fifteen federal meant he must have turned a good few people over, and in between his stoical acceptance of death he kept insisting that I come to San Sebastián and live with him and just in time for the running of the bulls and how we'd hunt wild boar with his dogs and a knife and the gypsy girls on the beach and his father's old fishing boat and kilos of hash and how syringes were free at the pharmacia. They took him on the third of July 1998 two days before they came for me.

I want to tell you how heroin saved my life, how my ability for self destruction has made of me a superior being apart and above the common run of man, of IT technicians and real estate brokers, of the smug smiles of once-born academics and even the petty betrayals of my former associates, I am above and hovering near the ceiling like a spirit at the demise of the body in which it formerly dwelt, free to bask in the unfolding separation of eternity. I was the golden child, I still am (aren't we all?) but the gradual realization that others did not always perceive this became the petrol that sparked my descent.

I grew up in East Africa in the sixties, at the end of the colonial dream, my parents part of the long tradition of peasants who dispersed to all parts of the Colonies in an attempt to escape the fate that awaited them at home, and in so doing aspired to become the very people they thought they had eluded, isn't life grand? There's always a chuckle behind the curtains. Our house in Dar es Salaam was on the edge of the Indian Ocean, when the tide was high waves lashed into the caves that dotted the shore and spouts of water would shoot up through portals that ran through their ceilings. I would lie in bed at night and time my breath to coincide with the explosion of the waves as if I and the ocean were one and between us we would birth strange gods.

We went to the cinema on Saturday afternoons to see *The Sound of Music* or *Chitty Chitty Bang Bang* and would walk down a dusty street filled with leprous beggars holding out bowls between two stumps, I would lift my ice cream close to my mouth for my tongue to lick as old men with elephantiasis pushed wheelbarrows by that housed their testicles swollen to the size of water melons and albino children stared blankly out of the darkened doorways of the hovels in which they dwelt. I recall my mother's hand stiffly propelling me down the street towards our destination protected by the regal shadows of a dying empire.

You cannot trust your memory, it lies, but you can trust your scars. I was raised by Edisa my black, black nanny, in a photograph of us there is me the golden child and there is the beautiful blackness that envelopes me punctuated by perfect white teeth and eyeballs, I am leaning sideways like a surfer on the wave of her arms safe that I am free to perform because I am adored. For Edisa I would practise my Swahili swearing, comunuoko, coumanima (mother fucking father fucking mother fucking bitch etc. etc.) and duly be chased through the house by a furious hornet clasping a stick and shaking with rage. When I was bored I sat at the screen door with a carving knife cutting off the tails of lizards who ventured inside to escape the heat, the sound of the chopping would draw her to me, if that didn't work I would stick a fork into the plug sockets on the wall and fly back screaming when the voltage came, the dry pop and the smoke announcing my presence. In the evenings I would sometimes escape from the house and find my way to the old concrete cowshed in which she lived in the back garden and sit quietly on the rolled mattress as she cooked strange stews on a gas ring that we ate with dough balls and fingers. Then I would lean into her warmth as she rocked us back and forth singing hushed songs to ward away demons.

PHOTOGRAPH:
Night, a cheap motel room, the United States.

A young Filipino drug dealer preparing to go to work stands in front of a full length mirror, he is combing his hair straight back, around his bare chest is a shoulder holster and pistol, a cigarette hangs from his lips, in the mirror you can see his prostitute girlfriend lying on a clothes-strewn bed watching him with admiration.

PHOTOGRAPH:
The living room of an apartment, the barrio,
San Francisco.

Blankets are nailed to all the windows, a single light bulb illuminates a gaunt man sitting on a stool. He is naked except for a white pair of boxer shorts, he is injecting himself in his right arm but his attention is not on this, around his head is a contraption made from jeweller's glasses and Velcro, a small metal arm juts out from the left of this machine on which a safety pin has been glued, on the end of the pin he has impaled a cockroach. Focus... shoot... wait...

My mother worked in Dar as a secretary for the East African Cotton Company and as such we were entitled to spend weekends in the beach house they owned on Pemba Island 20 miles from Zanzibar. A short ferry ride in my father's white Saab, some windy dust roads and you were there, there it is on the ridge to the right of the perfect white beach that slopes gently to the water line, there's a coral reef half a mile out that makes the entire bay a swimming pool of a thousand treasures. I spent whole days in these waters with my mask and spear gun or following my father's friends 'uncle' Mike and 'uncle' Steve as they harpooned barracuda and moray eel in the rocks of the reef, a rope tied to my ankle which led to the inner tube and net in which the catch was placed a crimson cloud of blood trailing in my wake. Just past the reef the ground dropped away to infinity, this was the land of sharks and vertigo, the place where I first tasted the boundlessness of terror that staked a place in my eight-year-old heart.

Gabriel, 2007
98 × 139 cm

At the Feet of the Empress, 2006
157 × 115 cm

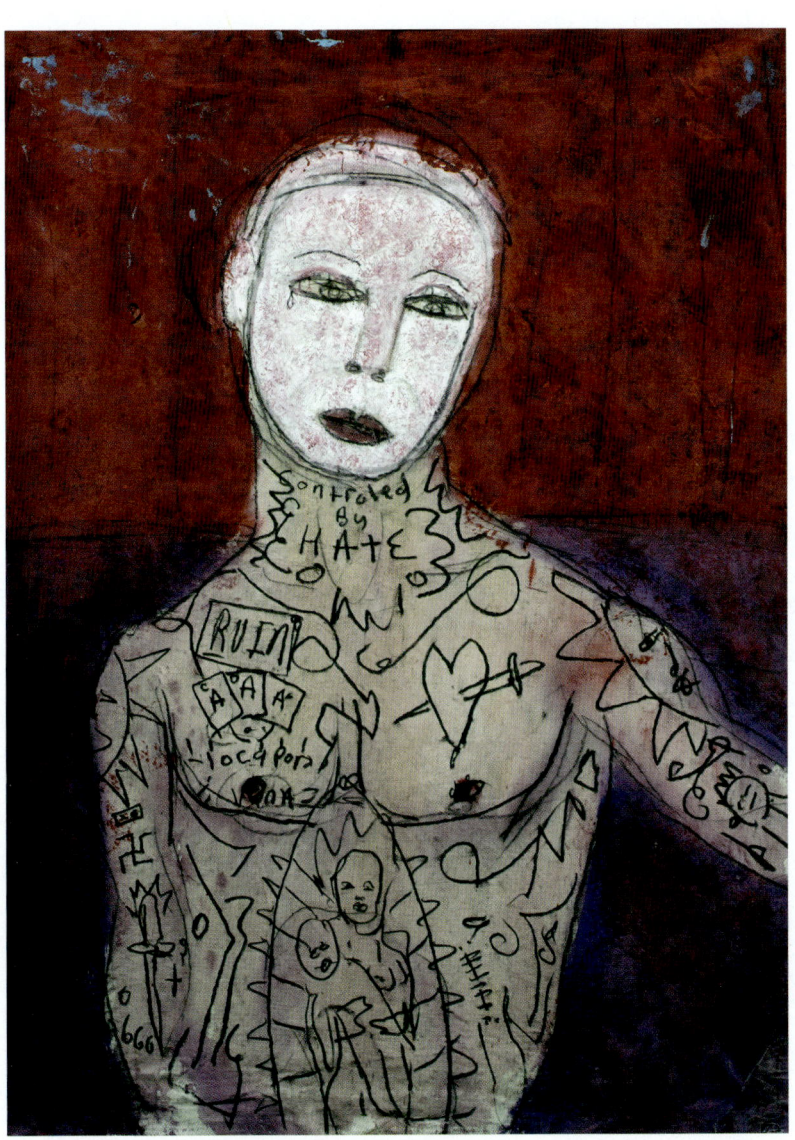

St Genet, 2008
100 × 140 cm

Regina's New Stockings, 2007
118 × 160 cm

Enough already, enough about Africa and sentiment and Christopher Robin, we all think we are holy as children, what about the knife that's got your name on it dancing up the alley at dawn twelve dollars clutched in your right hand and an old leather jacket so thick that that fucker can't get the blade to slide through, so you're just spinning circles together 'til he starts aiming for your head then you drop him and together you're rolling on the sidewalk as pedestrians walk silently by heading for work or the motel door that came crashing down as the San Francisco Parole Department stamps a boot on your face and jams a gun barrel to the back of your head as you furiously work your throat up and down trying to swallow those last two rocks that could cost you five more years because of your priors or the blank look on the face of your crimey as you stand above him with a claw hammer in your hand and explain to him the urgency that is required of him to hand over his share of the loot as you've spent yours already and all of the pipes have been pushed clean as whistles or the time you tried to kick smack on angel dust and you stood naked on the bed staring at the mirror convinced you could peel the skin from your head to your toes and a new creature would emerge shining and pink and free and how you walked out of the motel took a left and disappeared into another world that turned the piss of Sixth and Mission into the fragrance of roses…

America the beautiful god kept me company for 28 years hunting rattlesnakes in the Indian fields behind the Eichler homes that curved in monotony upon the crest of the San Mateo highlands. America where my father fell apart and turned to drugs and pornography as he tried to form a personality beneath the kind veneer, America where my crowning glory was the time I spent in solitary in the psychiatric maximum security wing at San Quentin as they tried to figure out if I'd been pushed or jumped from the third tier of west block my jaws wired together again and a copy of *Death in the Afternoon* to keep me company. It is the wastelands I remember, the San Gabriel mountains still echoing to the songs of Charles Manson, the desert and silver Airstream campers with ephedrine tanks and Harleys and runaway girls hitchhiking from Salinas to Hollywood, the ones who made it and the ones who didn't.

Rita was a classic case of fucking everybody because her rich daddy didn't care.

When I read her diary of her time in New York at 18 I got that washing machine stomach that I knew so well. "Went to the Peppermint Lounge, fucked a guy in the toilet then went to the hotel with the band and gave De De a blowjob", "March 19th got drunk at Danceteria and ended up fucking the cab driver in the back seat on the way to Tommy's house, passed out and woke up in Central Park with some black guy feeding me coke and fingering me on the bench outside MOMA, run out of money, daddy's ignoring my phone calls, going to Bermuda on Monday with Armand and Xavier, I miss my kitty I hope she's alright." I met Rita in '87 at some private record release gig in a Potrero Hill studio, she was wandering around with an unopened bottle of red wine in her hand asking boys if they had a corkscrew, I said I didn't but I'll get one. When she drove us to her apartment in Piedmont she told me to steer as she closed her eyes and stepped on the gas.

So I'm 10 and I'm perfect and I'm plucked from my reverie of lepers and mystery and dropped into the new land, Century City, Los Angeles County. It's 1971 and we're in some shitty apartment with mummy doing our lessons while outside mobs of people wearing tear gas masks and burning flags roll down the pavement. I don't know about Vietnam or politics or the fact that not all blacks are meant to be servants I just know that I'm trapped in a bubble looking out and I can't participate, I'm under house arrest and I don't yet understand what crime I've been charged with.

I have had to work hard to bring myself back, to retrain my thoughts and catch the snake of my damage as it awakens and slithers between my partner and me, if I'm not careful the finger I put in her mouth for her to suck as we make love will turn into the cock of my enemies, it wont be me she's fucking but all my best friends and like some tacky bukkake porn flick, in my rage, she only cums when there's six cocks slapping against her face. So yes at an early age I got sex and betrayal all stuck together and I've needed a scalpel to cut them apart. I am my own surgeon, who better for the job?

    I first started cutting myself at 11, I wasn't a dedicated cutter, it was more of an occasional performance than a full time commitment, but it seemed to accomplish its task. I like the sight of my blood, everything gets focused and holy and all of your doubts slip away. You are the architect of your destiny, you have taken control and there's only you and the limits of your pain to negotiate, no stepmothers who decide whether or not to give you a hand job tonight 'cos daddy's away, no stepfathers who hunt you down at night 'cos you've run away again and he's paid your buddies five dollars to tell him whose garden you're sleeping in and no dour mothers who look at you as if you are some strange alien that was planted in her womb for her sins and now you're just in the way, but don't get me wrong if there is such a thing as sin, self-pity is its seed, and pettiness the garden that it spawns. We are better than that, we love our betrayers and honour the scars of experience, but you gotta pay attention.

Rita was a runaway, she'd left Kansas City at 15 after she'd got drunk at a party and some boy had gotten her to give him a blowjob while the other kids were watching and now they called her "Hedda" and laughed when she went to school, so she packed a bag and hitchhiked to Seattle where her father lived only she didn't get to him she met Craig instead.

I want to pretend this is a love story, that something honourable can be found in a broken mess.

Left right uppercut duck and bang I'm almost 12 and I'm a fighter, after Russell Hirsh tried to push in front of me in the line at recess and I decked him. I discovered the joys of physical combat, slap fighting wrestling full contact mayhem but always with an audience, I've always liked the spectators but the thing is I have this weird version of the Marquess of Queensberry rules in my head so when Jamie Fenwick goes down from a punch and I help him up I'm disgusted when he knocks my legs out with a sweep and starts biting my face. I had this vision of myself as a gentleman thug and that's a hindrance, it's part of the masquerade of trying to create a personality for others to appreciate and it diminishes your strength. It wasn't until I smashed a bottle in a bar in Greece and tried to cut Joshua's throat that I understood the difference between truth and camouflage and that truth wins out every time.

Have you ever killed anyone? I don't think I have, not on purpose anyway but it's been close. One day you come up against some immoveable force and it just so happens that right now you're all present and accounted for and your eyes burn into each others and everything goes silent like it's holy hour and you know there's no turning back and you're scanning for spikes on the railings to impale his head on 'cos you don't have your crowbar and his fists are pumping to the rhythm of his heart and people start to back away and you remember how clean it felt when you were about to hang yourself and you summon that moment and he can see, he can tell that someone's going to die and for some reason he tries to laugh and offers you a cigarette which you take without speaking then he turns and walks slowly down the street back to the hostel where he gets drunk and picks up a fire extinguisher and crushes Drunk Tom the wet-brained Irish boy's skull to a pulp then lies down on the pool room floor and goes to sleep.

Each moment breeds a new universe we walk around blindly singing our future into being with every action we take or run from, isn't that great? Relax, there's no escape.

Let me explain.

So I'm in solitary at the San Quentin psychiatric wing I got a nice little cell to myself with a slot I can look through and see the ferries coming from San Fran to Sausalito. I can see the seagulls flying in the wind and watch the mud coming up from the floor of the bay in circles when the tide is full, I've got my copy of Hemingway and a wired jaw and two broken ribs, I gotta shackle up backwards two times a week for my shower when I get to see my neighbours for a heartbeat, on the left some fat guy with long black hair and a beard is chained lying on a metal table inside a glass cell for maximum observation, he smiles as I'm led by. On the right is wolf boy who bangs his head and eats his own shit, they have to tear gas him and strap him to a pole by his wrists and feet like a stuck pig to take him for medical 'cos he's not complying, not one little bit, stay down wolf boy, so it's OK in here like some bad dream where you're not afraid but I'm hungry, in fact I'm starving and this liquid diet of pureed potatoes and water sucked through a straw is not hitting the spot and when the cops bring me chow they laugh and make slurping sounds 'cos that's what they hear coming out of my cell, my jaw is wired tight, sealed shut and I'm in that post kicking phase where you just gotta eat anything that's not nailed down and I gotta get out of here and get some fucking chow. San Quentin is a medieval castle it's a paleolithic cave it's old school and you know you're in a fucking prison not some politicaly correct dorm with Nintendo and social workers. I'm just here waiting transportation to Norco again but I was so fucking dope sick I took a swan dive off the third tier to get some relief and they don't believe me, they think I've been pushed and there's some little gang affiliation drama to be had but I'm not in any gang, I'm solo and always have been.

Life's fantastic, it's like riding a Norton Commando down the Pacific coast highway with a runaway girl holding on tight, and you know that she loves you 'cos she does blowjobs at the truckstops in Modesto and Stockton and brings you the money so you can go get the heroin and cocaine and crack and brandy and when she's loaded all she does is paint angels and horses out of Dürer books in gold and silver and when you come out of prison again and make love to her she whispers "oh baby that feels like you" and you know that you're special 'cos she's fucked 10,000 guys since you've been away and every now and then you get a stolen moment when you get the balance of heroin and cocaine just perfect in that syringe and you find a fat new vein under your armpit and when you hit it a beautiful red river comes flooding into the barrel and you've paid two nights rent in this shitty motel 'cos you're thinking of the future now and you know that you're really an angel in disguise and one day the world will wake up and understand.

I did ten years with Rita, most of the time I was locked up, which might account for our longevity but nevertheless ten years is ten years but they merge into the ten years before and Rita turns into Lael or Annette or Melissa or Lisa or Odette or Monica and they merge with the ten years before and…

Melanie was 19 long straight blonde hair, slightly bucked teeth and a big nose but she was sexy. My father married her when I was 11 and she arrived in his Woodlake apartment for my new life of weekends with dad. She had a ceramic beerstein she had made in high school with the names of all the men she'd slept with inscribed on its sides. She used to pick me up on Friday afternoons and we'd go to the rec center to buy lids of pot from the high school boys, I felt so proud as we approached together, like she was mine and the other guys would notice me because of who I was with. The first time it happened we were on the couch watching the film *Bluebeard*, she was lying down with her legs on my knees, her shoes were off and out of nowhere I felt her stockinged heel start to dig circles and grind up my thigh when she got to my crotch and felt my little hard cock poking through my jeans she laughed looked me in the eyes and said "what's that, huh? what's that, huh?" That night was the first time I came, it like the first shot of cocaine, has never been quite the same. My head exploded in a cacophony of fireworks and tsunami waves and I realized that god was truly great. Sucker. Now I've got a problem, I love my dad, he smokes pot with me and sets up strobe lights in the living room and plays Kraftwerk trying to get a headrush, he sends away for African yohimbra bark and fly agaric from the back pages of *High Times* and tells me he's a cocksman and that no woman is to be trusted, they're all bitches like my mother and how he hates that fucking cunt she married, all good stuff, but the thing is I'm desperate for him to fuck off again so Melanie will get bored and put her hand down my trousers, for her to laugh and squeeze my little cock and guide my hand between her legs and show me how to rub figure eights around her pussy lips as she plays Super 8 porn films and shows me the drawer full of dildos and wigs and fucked up magazines dad's getting from Amsterdam and Stockholm and how from the age of 8 her two brothers used to sneak in her room at night and touch her all over and rub their cocks around her pussy (they never put them all the way in) and how my dad's got the fattest prick she's ever seen and when he covers it in Vaseline and puts it up her ass it pops out clean as a whistle.

We are plants programmed to feed and propagate, life is just a veiled performance dedicated to the gathering of nutrients and the division of cells, we are property, we are cattle on the cosmic farm and nature plays with loaded dice.

One night Melanie came home with her boss from work, she was a secretary at Envirotech, a company that processed America's shit, and with her was this man. We drank wine and smoked pot and she played her *Goodbye Yellow Brick Road* and Boston, *More Than a Feeling*, then pulled out the sofa bed. The three of us were lying on it, Melanie in the middle, I was on the left and then she rolled over putting her back to me and started kissing this fucking invader. I was raging but determined so I stuck my hands down the back of her stockings and started fingering the first available hole, which was just as well 'cos the one in front was occupied by the hand of this bastard who was doing my girl, in fact my dad's wife, right in front of my eyes, then they get up and leave together and it's just me and my aching little balls waiting for the key to turn in the latch. There are times in life when we birth new creatures inside of ourselves, when little wet demons first blink their eyes and start smacking their lips in order to be fed. So now I'm the jealous boy, I got an insight on girls, just like my dad, I know you're gonna betray me you bitch so just get it over with and bring home some cash. Melanie became a Christian ha ha ha, twenty years later I get a letter in prison saying I'm sorry and praise the lord but you know I'd much rather she bent down so I could fuck her properly and even out the scales. I threw away the letter.

PHOTOGRAPH:
Time unknown.

Foreground, a young man shirtless, tattooed, faces a mirror with his teeth bared, metal wires are entwined through his teeth to clamp his jaws together, in his right hand, which is raised to his mouth, he holds a red-handled pair of wire cutters.

PHOTOGRAPH:
Colour.

Top of the frame a girl's bowed head, her left arm extends to the forefront, it is covered in a series of precise lacerations, in her right hand she holds a pair of surgical tweezers with which she is pulling from one of the lacerations a small green aphid.

Let's stop being coy, I know god or whatever the fuck you want to call the feeling that rises up out of the blades of grass that you're meant to be weeding as punishment for eternity in the field behind the house, the Indian field, he-she rises up through tears of rage and the lumps of dirt you've been eating to make yourself choke. The devil is a raging bull from Sicily and he sticks his tongue in your mother's mouth and works it back and forth, he sentences you to hard labour for life without the possibility of parole and you're too frightened to fight him and haven't yet mastered the arts of running away so all you can do is self implode. God is the clear stillness that brings the cracks in the dirt to life and pulls you down through your eyes into ancient lands that surround us beneath and above. It is the burning of the dross 'til there's nothing left but your breath and the beat of your heart and suddenly everything's perfect and still and you can't remember why you've been crying or what for, it's just the blue ocean of a sky and your god is your mother's fingers stroking your hair as you lie in her lap overdosed on codeine and sliced arm to arm, god is the strength you find to dive through the plate glass window with cop cars outside the front of the house and you fly over the fence and into the fields it's raining at night and your father's been summoned as a last resort and instead of beating the devil he whips you with his belt, buckle first, in the house that used to be his in front of the wife that used to be his and he's calling your name saying I'm sorry I'm sorry but it's too late, you're finally free to run, covered in blood and blessed long gone into the wastelands. God has a dim sister and heroin is her name.

I'm the runaway boy, life only happens for me when I get the courage to climb out of my rescuer's window, shimmy down the drainpipe and hit the streets on my own.

Alfredo taught me how to steal, he was a Puerto Rican Indian with pockmarks and a blonde hooker girlfriend who looked like my blonde hooker girlfriend so we had something in common. He put his jacket over his shoulder and said "just watch". He strolled into Gap on Market Street, picked up a pile of blue jeans, stuck them between his arm and his ribs and sauntered out the door. Then he handed me the jacket and said "OK huero, your turn". For six months I was untouchable. The jackets turned into flash trenchcoats and the piles of merchandise started popping out the sides as I strolled like a ghost through the exits and into the getaway cars. I had different drivers for different runs, sometimes I'd stay local and send in some street freak to draw security first and I'd slide in and out like the invisible man, that was the idea and it worked fine 'til the day I came out of Sears in San Bruno and got smashed to the asphalt by Starsky and Hutch. It hurts to find out you're only human, you're just like all the rest and sometimes you can't even make that mark. You become desperate and vicious when cornered, you develop a set of camouflages for every occasion until there's not much left of you that you even recognise and the bottom line of your existence is the constant terror of being dope sick.

Heroin and crack are gifts to be imbued by the children of the wealthy, in the arms of the poor they just become another degradation, the poor know reality, the rich have to be taught in order to become human, the perimeter of the compound has to be breached with an overdosed heir on his 21st birthday, or photographs of Camilla just turned 15 smoking crack with the ghost of Tupac's dick up her ass. Pain is the great leveller, anguish is the field where we all unite in the moment, stripped of the accoutrements of culture and style, knowledge and power, in disaster we are born as the lambs from the scriptures, if only for a moment.

So I'm a junky, I'm a scumbag, I'm a crackhead, I'm the piece of shit you walk by sitting on the curb between two cars stamping cottons in a dirty cooker at 7 a.m. a crowbar wrapped to my left calf beneath my trousers, I'm the dog who haunts the fag boutiques on Castro Street armed with a syringe full of blood "I've got AIDS motherfucker, back up or I'll stab you" then loads up on Calvin Klein and Levi's 501s and runs out the door, back down to the barrio to the 24-hour donut shop on 18th and Mission where the El Salvadorian fences buy everything American and out of nowhere you got a hundred bucks and Rita's still sleeping at the Royan Hotel on 16th and Valencia. She doesn't know you took the last twenty dollars at 3 a.m., the money for the wake up shot, you took it like a surgeon out of her pussy where she'd hidden it so you wouldn't rob her again, you could get back in time, she wouldn't even know, but you, you just keep shooting speed-balls and smoking rocks up and down the streets 'til you come to without a shirt and filthy with your head in a garbage can 'cos you know someone must have dropped a rock in here and now you're too fucking freaked to do any more crime so you slink back to the motel and pretend to be sleeping 'til she wakes up crying and sick and has to go out snot running out of her nose to give some Mexican a blow job in the alley so she can get well and start it again.

It wasn't always like this. When I first got with Rita I'd just kicked my first bad habit on my brother's couch in Redwood City. I was young and soft and hadn't yet understood the nature of reality. I was probably just like you.

The first time I did a trick I was 15. I was hitchhiking from San Francisco to LA and a silver Peugeot pulled over just outside San Jose and an old man with elegant fingers pushed open the passenger door. Who cares if some faggot is sucking your cock in his car at the McDonalds parking lot outside Salinas, you just ate two cheeseburgers and he's given you twenty bucks so you close your eyes and think of Sydney Lee Rhodes and going bareback on the ponies at midnight out to the reservoir where you swam naked and she grabbed your head underwater and stuck your face straight into her blonde pussy.

PHOTOGRAPH:
Evening.

> Monterey pier, interior of a camper van shot from the front, and in the background on both sides of the van are piled cages containing dogs. In the driver's seat an overweight man leans over the thighs of a young boy, one hand is pulling up the boys white t-shirt, the boy's head is tilted back staring at the roof, his right arm rests outside the passenger window, a burning cigarette between two fingers.

"Are you a faggot white boy?"

"No I swear to god."

"So why'd you let that queer suck your dick?"

"'Cos I needed the cash."

"Oh yea what about that old man you fucked in the ass?

"Aw shit, I had to have a Hustler magazine stuck on his back or else it just wasn't happening."

"Well my homey says he seen you in a porn film and you looked like you was having a good time."

"Ah well that boy was kinda cute, anyway aren't you the motherfucker who used to screw chickens on the farm in Oaxaca? And your dad beat your ass 'cos he'd come into the barn in the morning and all the chickens were dead? Ha! Shut the fuck up Topo and deal the cards."

Buffalo taught me how to play pinochle at CRC in '92, he said it would take four straight days but we did it in three. Ten jack queen king ace out of the four suits little joker and the big joker makes 82 cards, to play with the big boys you have to be aware of them all. Your partner shoots you meld in increments of one for ten starting from 50 so 53 would be 30 meld and you bid counting your meld and his, say 65, and the difference between your total meld and your bid is the amount of tricks you have to take with a minimum of twenty, so if I bid 65 and together we have 35 meld that means we have to pull thirty tricks or we are set, two sets is game over a pinochle is when you pull every trick on the table.

I've done it twice and as you get closer to the holy grail other cons drift over 'cos they can feel what's happening, you're just about there and your table is surrounded in a silent reverie, everyone's watching how you're playing your hand, you've almost run out of trumps but your partner's taken the hearts with a queen and come back to you in trumps so you know he's got the hearts all sewn up and you can smell it, you've got four garbage cards one trump and a jack of hearts, play your last trump and drop the jack, yea he's in control now and runs those hearts down standing on top of his chair screaming "give me your shit motherfucker!" and slamming his daddies to the table "who's your fucking daddy bitch!" slam and you're echoing "you're the man you bad motherfucker!" and there it is, pinochle, every fucking trick on the table and the crowd starts clapping and even the losers are honoured to have witnessed this great event and it's count time so you pick up the case of soup you won and walk back to your bunk on the air.

Buffalo was an old con, he looked like Wild Bill Hickok on a bad day, six two, 240 pounds long brown grey hair and a big handlebar moustache, he used to carry around an ancient coffee mug he never washed in his nicotine-stained fingers, he'd say "you never know when things are gonna dry up, dog" meaning if he ran out of coffee he could scrape the sides of his mug like you pound an old cotton.

Buffalo taught me the basics, never walk around with your toothbrush in your mouth 'cos someone could jam it down your throat, how we keep old newspapers to roll up and line the insides of our jackets in case it went down and people started getting stabbed, how to melt the end of a plastic fork and line it with razors, when you're at chow stare straight

PCP, 2009
145 × 165 cm

Forth Worth Texas, 2008
125 × 158 cm

Another Blue Sky, 2010
121 × 156 cm

Hosanna, 2011
118 × 152 cm

ahead and — the holy commandment — never smoke after or eat anything off a black man's tray. But none of this means anything in the end all it does is provide you with a society where people think twice before mouthing off, where the potential repercussions of carnage are enough to make the clever dicks from the street hold their tongue. That's part of the reason I liked prison so much, you didn't have to put up with the petty bullshit of society and when something did go down you knew it was going to be real.

Enough already. Fuck another prison book, I mean I love Chopper and Papillon and Dostoyevsky and *Moments of Reprieve* by Primo Levi, I know solitary confinement is a wonderful place to breathe in and the thrill it is to be paraded through public in a full set of shackles and an armed escort, I can even get carried away and wax lyrical about the strange silence that ensues after the blue light above north block in San Quentin goes out and you know they just executed some mongrel and tomorrow we'll be off lockdown after three days in our cells or the dumb look of pride on the cons' faces as they scream dead man walking and you're supposed to stop cold and face the wall as they escort Richard Ramirez "The Night Stalker" to the law library, he's got on mirrored shades and looks like a rock star surrounded by groupies. Yes, we're all stupid cunts. In prison you eat, shit and piss like you do in your penthouse, you breathe, you wank, you tell lies and your nightmares are the same ones you had as a child, the images change but the sins remain the same, the only difference is in prison you don't have to do anything about it, you are back in the womb, you are safe from the horrors of facing up to your own ineptness and confusion, everything's simplified. For me it was easier to be stabbed than to get a job or pay the rent. I didn't realise that my perceived weakness was really my strength, an absolute refusal to do anything that did not please me, but when that pleasing takes the form of destruction and rage it gets complicated.

I have a big cock. I'm sure there are bigger ones but mine's not bad, I didn't do anything to deserve it, it just comes with the package so I realize there's nothing to be proud of but it helps pay the rent in so many words. When I first went to America and had to shower with the other boys after gym I realised I was different. They were all circumcised. I looked like I had a little elephant's trunk down there while they had helmets of varying hues. I was never teased but its potential was enough for me to refuse to go back to gym. After missing enough sessions the school rang my mother who sat me down and asked me what the problem was. I told her and she and my stepfather came up with the solution of getting me circumcised at 11. I accepted and when I returned from the hospital picked out my stitches which left holes that are still visible.

These were my first scars. So out of nowhere here comes this crippling shame, or perhaps it was being bred for 11 years and just found the right time to pop up and say "hello you freaky little germ hide thy self and tremble at my feet" it was like I manifested the whole expulsion from Eden in my little boy world without ever reading the Bible, my neck turned crimson when I felt exposed, I'd rather shit in my pants than use the open toilet on my first school camping trip and my hand would tremble when lighting another kid's cigarette. So my life has been a head-on collision with shame. I have been impelled again and again to have my face rubbed in its fat breasts until finally I hold the upper hand, that's what a hundred strip searches and eating out of garbage cans have given me, a tentative victory over my perceived demons and the ability to bend over, spread my ass cheeks and laugh as I fart for the prison guards.

When I was 15 my stepfather got tired of hunting me in ravines and dragging me to school by my hair. We'd battled for four years and the little boy thought he had slain the Minotaur so I was dispatched to the cheapest boarding school they could find which turned out to be Midlands in the Santa Ynez valley, 40 miles from Santa Barbara, an old ranch with wood cabins and horses and Indian mounds and 3000 acres of forests and mountains and as the gods would have it the year I arrived was the first year that Midland had girls.

I met you at the Mardi Gras, on a French Quarter sidewalk, when you kissed me it was strong, I wonder if you hear this song.

Sydney Lee Rhodes was a wild child. When I arrived at Midlands there were three girls on bedrest with genital herpes, stung by Sydney's fat pouting lips. By day she claimed Mark Brandon and Greg Goode as her boyfriends, by night she'd sit outside the English master's office cabin summoning him with her flute, Sydney Lee — she had long blonde hair matted like a stallion's tail, her breasts were full moons topped with nipples that saluted the stars and when she looked at you all you saw were two brown eyes that lived on an LSD damaged planet where all you did was fuck. Yes I'm a romantic fool but she really was Aphrodite and the Magdalene and the foam of creation bubbled out from her blonde pussy lips. She led me by the hand to an old tree fort and spent an hour sucking my balls and from that point my sole purpose was to steal alcohol from faculty homes and ride out bareback at night with Sydney to celebrate the pagan gods. From Sydney I got a master's degree in sex and damage, from Midlands I just got expelled. I didn't have a home as far as I was concerned so when the school put me on a bus to San Francisco for my third offence of burgling faculty homes I jumped off in Salinas and hitchhiked to Monterey where I knew a kid who lived with his crazy mum who might take in a stray.

All I remember of Monterey was the pier, Steinbeck's *Cannery Row* transported to 1977 with seafood restaurants and marine cruises in place of the canning factories of the thirties, but his people were still there, the hobos and winos and drifters still flowed in and out like they had for a hundred years. I got a job washing dishes in a big Italian crab and steak house and at night after my shift I'd get a big tub of steaks and crablegs I'd collected from the leftovers on the plates I washed and take them down to the campfires under the pier, these were my people and though I didn't understand why I do now. Brown leather faces toothless grins missing fingers, crutches and stray dogs drinking Ripple and Thunderbird and Rainer

Ale, these guys still rode the freight trains from Salt Lake City and Chicago and Albuquerque, they talked about beaches in Mexico where they spent the winter and picking grapes in the Napa Valley. I felt like Jim out of *Treasure Island* and this pirate crew made a place for me at the campfire and handed me half a warm Colt 45.

Stevie was a runaway, he was blond with a girl's blue eyes and at around midnight he'd go up to the pier and come back in an hour with sixty bucks. One night he took me with him, that's where I learned how to stand with one leg propped on the railings one hand in your pocket the other holding a cigarette to your mouth while staring into the approaching cars' windscreens like you were the ghost of James Dean. (*I am the passenger and I ride and I ride I ride out through the city at night oh the bright and hollow sky I see the city's ripped backsides la la la la le la* I don't remember the words but it's so fucking true la la la.) Most of the men who stopped were OK, they probably had been lying in bed next to their wives unable to sleep and for whatever reason decided to take twenty bucks down to the pier and suck a young boy's dick then drive home and quietly slip back beneath the covers with a gentle kiss on their wife's sleeping shoulder, who knows I don't care, I've got things to do and I'm definitely not washing any more fucking dishes.

"Welcome to Whataburger, can I take your order?" "Yeah, ahl have a triple patty wit cheese jalapenos sour cream ketchup and a jumbo chocolate shake." Dallas, Texas, is butt ugly and flat as a transvestite's chest, Sid Vicious just died on the radio and dad's sent me a ticket 'cos the nice lady in Monterey kicked me out 'cos I drink a bit. I'm flipping patties nights in Whataburger in Garland and fucking Tania and Trixie, two sisters from Louisiana. They introduce me to Armando and Michael, these guys are about 18 but seem all grown up to me. They live in the Lazy Eight Motel, drive a metallic green 452 Monte Carlo and sell big bags of Oaxaca buds soaked in PCP that they bring back from El Paso. Armando's got this stunning girl who's a stripper and they sit in their room cleaning their shotguns and counting money just like in the movies. So I'm in the gang, I help bag up and order food from the Mexican restaurant to be delivered, we drink whiskey and coke by the swimming pool. At night we drive around and Armando drops off duffle bags of sherm to motel doors that look just like our motel door then we get arrested in a bowling alley parking lot 'cos Armando shot at a car that was following us. I'm fucked up on PCP but still hold my wits and tell the officer at Dallas County Jail I was just hitchhiking and have no idea what's going on. Four days later at my court appearance I'm ordered out of the state of Texas, well thank you, sir, thank you very much.

So like I said I am the passenger, I climb into cars that someone else is driving, I have no destination or purpose I just tag along like a ghost that lingers on other people's trajectories. Josh and Reg were two brothers from London I'd met at Midlands boarding school. Their mother Ginny had died of cancer and their dad, Marvin, had remarried and moved from Highgate to the Hollywood hills. Marvin's wife

Alison was minted, she was old school East Coast money, and Marvin had been Mr Photographer for Francis Coppola, he did the stills for *Apocalypse Now* and had *Life* magazine credentials so blah blah blah I call Josh and he says "come and live with us". OK. Marvin and Alison have bought three houses in the Hollywood Hills, one the family live in and the other two Marvin's rebuilding using slave labour from the Tenderloin, his kids and now me. Fucking cool. Josh and I live in our own four-bedroom palace off Mulholland, we have a swimming pool and a jacuzzi and Marvin lives next to Ringo on Torreyson Drive. He feeds the whole crew and brings cases of beer at five o'clock and always has a joint in his mouth, not bad for a ghost. Hollywood was good to me, and I worked my ass off for Marvin, chopping hills in half to lay railroad ties and brick patios in a hundred degrees in July, Doc Marten boots and cut off jeans, I learned to acid-wash swimming pools and paint them with thermal paint and I found joy in being given a hammer and crow bar and being pointed in the direction of a large structure and urged to destroy. I sure as fuck couldn't build it but I was good at tearing it down.

There are times when I look back and think I could have stayed, I could have made a stand and things would be different but if everything is perfect now what the fuck does it matter.

Damage has followed me like a shadow that draws forth all the damned fish in god's ocean, I am the piper whose flute brings forth crippled children who dance with me while the world revolves in its sleep. Fiona gave me syphilis and gonorrhea. I had been warned but I was always drunk and didn't care anyway, a Greek cop in Lindos said she used to come to the station and fuck the policemen on the roof late at night and they'd all got the clap from her, but when she'd arrive at 3 a.m. at my spot on the beach and climb into my sleeping bag stinking of alcohol I think she just wanted to be held, we all just want to be held but fucking seems to be the only way some people can express it.

Erik was from Sweden. When I met him he had on buckskin trousers, old cowboy boots, an Afghani vest and a long silk scarf with a print of Kali the goddess of destruction up and down both sides. He was sporting two silver bangles cast from a human skull in Benares on each wrist. He was lying on the black tiles of Jules's Chelsea flat coming in and out of an overdose. Jules opened the door to me and said "darling get him out of here, he's such a mess." Eric had just done 36 hours on flights from Bangkok to Heathrow after Teddy his sugar daddy had bailed him out of a prison in northern Thailand. His right arm was seized up like a claw from a muscle shot and his light blue eyes went in opposite directions each time he came to, when he'd keep laughing and saying "it's so good, it's so good".

Eric gave me my first taste of heroin. Jules didn't like heroin, she liked champagne and fucking young boys. She picked me up on a beach in Greece at 18 where I'd been scavenging dinners off restaurant customer's plates and passing out in the sand bloated on Metaxa and Ouzo. I was walking by her in a bar and she stuck her fingers in the beltloop of my jeans and said "hello you, what's your name?" She was doing that vampire flamenco dancer thing with dyed black hair and spangled stilettos. She flew me back to London and introduced me to the world of contrived decadence which has always been around when people have too much, it was London 1979, Derek Jarman, Andrew Logan, the Blitz Kids, St Martins and art pretending to be in Caligula's court, it was contrived and as fraudulent as the ruffles on Marie Antoinette's skirts but it wasn't 'til I saw the Virgin Prunes at the Lyceum and met some people from Killing Joke that I realized something stronger ran like a river beneath the froth of civilization.

Jules couldn't cum, no matter how many boys she fucked it just wasn't happening, I kinda wish I could go back 30 years and give it another go, making her cum I mean, fuck living with her she was a nightmare but beautiful. The streets parted as she went by with her elegant corruption. At the dinner party where we met her ex Daniel and his new girlfriend Lesley she made a point of ceremoniously leading me by the hand to the toilet and squatting on the rim while I fucked her then she smoothed out her gypsy dress and led me back to the table like Salome holding out the head of John the Baptist for the court to admire, like I said, girls don't you just love 'em.

When you first use heroin you puke holy water and your cock is a mountain with deep roots when you fuck you're as strong as a Lipizzaner stallion and you grind against her pelvic bone like tectonic plates mashing in the Marshall Trench but it doesn't last. You've got probably two weeks of daily using 'til the tables turn and the horse is riding you. So what I do know is that London, New York and San Francisco all merged into a five-year haze of transvestite drug dealers, Jules's fashion shoots, brandy and champagne. Jules paid for everything and slowly it took its toll on me, she'd set up job interviews for me and give me some money each morning and I'd spend the day in cinemas watching *Les Enfants du Paradis* or Kurusowa films and tell her lies about the job that was coming up, I didn't want to work, I didn't want to do anything but be taken care of but for me being taken care of is the kiss of death.

I wanna talk about betrayal, I wanna talk about the first time I stole money from my mother's purse when I was 10 and when she opened it she cried 'cos they were the last dollars we had 'cos she'd just kicked my father out and we needed it for food. I had spent it with Richard Lebis, paid him my mum's last 10 dollars for a bagful of pot seeds. He'd ripped me off but I didn't quite understand yet, so she's crying and knows it's me and I just act dumb and pretend I don't know what she's talking about but she knew and so did I. So by the time I'm 12 I've got violations on nine of the ten commandments. I didn't have to be shown or indoctrinated by society they were just natural emotional reactions, so I'm an essentialist, I'm an animist, a vitalist even, I have a natural propensity for crime as a means of alleviating an unacceptable situation. I burgle houses I run away I take any drug I can find I finger paint with my blood and have sex with my father's wife. It wasn't until I read Jean Genet that I realized how blessed I was.

Uncle Dootie introduced me to the wonderful world of intravenous injections. Reggie and I had a band. It's San Francisco in the early eighties and Reggie had a black girlfriend from New York and Uncle Dootie was her older brother Warren. Warren was hip slick and cool, he had a James Dean pompadour made out of little dreads, youth authority tats on his arms and chest and he was tall and skinny and sharp as a razor kinda like a black Willy DeVille. So we're speeding away at the Vats south of Market at the old Hams brewery that's been taken over by the tribes playing 24 hours straight in one of the hundreds of torpedo tubes that used to be full of beer, Millions of Dead Cops are here, The Dicks, The Fuck-Ups, American Music Club, the original Faith No More. Marc Pauline and the Survival Research Laboratories are in the neighbourhood but all of this is about to disappear into the syringe full of cocaine Warren sticks into my arm between songs. Hey, we all line up like penguins with our sleeves rolled up and Warren does his little laugh like he's buttfucking you and you can't tell and hits us up, Jonny, Reggie, Becky, Gary from Oklahoma and me. Wow fucking hell that was even better than playing loud, now I'm doing the songs in a hurry so we can get another shot, in fact fuck the songs and the guitar let's just shoot up all the time oh boy oh boy oh boy hello! I'd just been a regular fellow before, I drank brandy and Rainer Ale snorted crystal meth and coke smoked chiva on tin foil and sometimes boiled it up and squirted it down my nose but all of that was kids' stuff compared to a direct hit of cocaine, and when you added some heroin to the mixture it was like going up in a rocket with a silk parachute that billowed out in perfect time to catch your cocaine crash.

So if you have a penchant for narcotics no money and refuse to work you need some girls in your life. Girls can make money quick and don't get locked up as frequently as boys. At first it's Lael, my father's third wife's best friend who I met on a cocaine weekend with dad in LA. When we started hanging out she's working in the epicure department in Neiman Marcus and is an upper-middle-class girl from Seattle whose dad is a bank manager. She held out her arm and I hit her up and the next thing you know she's waitressing at nights 'cos they get paid cash every 24 hours instead of once a month, then we give up her apartment and move into the Hotel Utah on Third Street 'cos it's so much cheaper and I figure out that if I send Lael over to Bobby's to score she comes back with a much bigger piece than I do. And then we start to overdose and I'm getting arrested in my hospital bed and we go to Mexico to get clean and I'm shooting coke in San Blas and hiding syringes all over town and we spend all the money and sell the car and crawl back to the border three months later and she's fucked she's broken. We get to San Francisco with no money and nowhere to live and she's sitting on her suitcase on Market Street crying and crying so I call mummy who calls Lael's daddy and breaks him the news that his daughter is a homeless heroin addict and she's putting her on a plane back to Seattle and she drops me on the couch at my brother's house in Redwood City to contemplate my next move. That's when I met Rita.

Driving a stolen car on a crime spree is like doing a Buddhist meditation on awareness. You fucking pay attention to everything around you, the rear view mirror the petrol gauge the little cooker full of heroin and coke by the gear shift you dip into at the red lights. You follow your breath and you sit up straight while driving 'cos you're fucking alive and this moment is all you've got.

Rita Rita pumpkin eater had a boy who sometimes beat her so she stabbed him in the arm and ran him over with her car, no it doesn't rhyme but twenty years later you want to say I'm sorry baby, I'm sorry, and to treat her with some grace but as you say I'm sorry you start to feel sorry for yourself and then you get confused and don't know who to blame or what the fuck happened or how you survived and if she's even alive.

Heroin's cheap in California, it comes in from the mountains of Sinaloa halfway between opium and china white, it's black tar and they call it chiva which translates as goat shit. You don't have to hit it with citric or do anything but put a little water and heat to it and it breaks down into a light brown syrup. Sometimes you get the black crystal variety which looks like Nescafé grinds and you blow a magic breath on it and it solidifies in front of your eyes, I've even run out of matches and just stuck a finger on top of a tenth and rubbed it around the cooker with 60 c.c. of water and it breaks down just from the heat of your skin.

Society has so many levels but underneath it all run the three

Gunas, they are the Vedic modes of being that are like oceans that sweep you along. Sattva sits on top, clear, calm and focused, then there's Raja, the land of action energy and intentions, and beneath them both is the turgid sea of Tapa, thick and inert, the mud of the graveyard where you walk in blind circles sinking deeper with every habitual step.

They had to hose me down, put my clothes in plastic bags with rubber gloves. My left big toe nail came off with the sock I prised from my foot and all the time I'm still thinking I'm a prince.

Rita knew the score, like I said she was a runaway at 15 and at 17 she did time for pandering and prostitution, then big daddy came to the rescue with a red jeep and an apartment in Seattle and method acting classes in Manhattan and his younger brother, Uncle Jim, had taken her to Bermuda for her 18th birthday and she fucked him on the beach, she laughed when she told me. At first she was mortified when she found out I'd been fixing her diet pills in the bathroom, she was pounding on the door screaming what the fuck are you doing so I open the door with a syringe in my hand and the cooker on top of the cistern and she says get out get out of here you fuck, so I grab my shirt and twenty dollars and I'm gone gone to the Tenderloin with a punk ass twenty gone to Mad Bob's on the 18th floor of the Eddy Street high-rise for the evacuees of the state mental hospitals, Bob is fat and stinks, the apartment is brown slime from floor to walls to ceilings black plastic bags full of old clothes he's taken from dumpsters fill the rooms, the kitchen is an ocean of stinking plates and tins and rotting food, Bob sits in a corner crying and laughing and talking to people who laugh at him then he snaps out long enough to go out and get us a one and one and I cook it up and give him a wet cotton.

Yea, heroin is a great leveller of social division, people you'd never cross swords with are suddenly put in your path and the little things that go up to create boundaries and tradition are kicked to the curb.

The Tenderloin in San Fran has a different odour of disease than the Mission, in the Tenderloin you can smell the HIV and despair in the piss that fills the street, old drunk Indians with cirrhotic livers bump into various stages of surgically-altered transvestites out catching tricks on the corners and skeleton speed couples zigzag their way to the liquor store trying to stay out of the sun. In the Tenderloin it's the Cambodians and Vietnamese who live side by side with the outcasts not the Mexicans and old school Irish who bring the Mission just a touch of community, the Tenderloin's more desperate like an old whore dying on a gurney in some hallway in General Hospital while the rest of the world walks by.

Rita always came for me no matter what I'd done, she'd eventually sacrifice what dignity she had, get in the Bronco and hunt me down, I could beat her rob her shoot all the drugs while she was sleeping and she'd still pull up outside whatever shithole I was hiding out in and honk the horn like an air raid siren 'til I came out, and then one day she didn't come.

You've got to be self-contained, you've got to be able to provide for yourself every bit of anything you require from the world each day, otherwise you'd just be lying in the crib crying for mummy to feed you and soon mummy's gonna hate your little ass almost as much as you hate yourself.

That's me in the piss alley behind the Royan Hotel on Valencia screaming up at the seventh floor window for my syringe full of heroin and coke to be thrown out post-haste, and nothing's happening, she's been in there with Jorge for two hours now and not a fucking glimmer for me, then the window opens and out come my shoes followed by a finger that points "fuck you" to the sky and the window slams shut, whaddaya know, the bitch has gone crazy. I sit down and contemplate my next move, it starts to rain so I put up an old piece of plywood against the wall and crawl behind it to wait, I fall asleep and wake up I fall asleep and wake up it's raining harder now it's fucking pouring and I'm getting sick and weak but I don't know what to do, I'm waiting for mummy to feed me, she always comes what the fuck is happening. I sat in that alley for 36 hours before I had the strength to let go and stand up on my own.

When Rita started doing tricks again I led the way. After ten years of retirement one morning we woke up with nothing left to sell and a big habit so she calls an escort service to sign onto their books and I head down to Polk Street to see if I

Midnight Rambler, 2009
107 × 132 cm

Pop Gun Robbery, 2008
120 × 141 cm

The Lolly Pop Girls Take Two, 2010
116 × 142 cm

The Parolees, 2006
113 × 157 cm

can still catch, it took me three hours to make 30 bucks and in that time Rita gets a phone call and an address and in 20 minutes she's got $250, fuck Polk Street she's a gold mine and good at her job and the money comes floating in and Pedro and his boys have keys cut for our door so they can deliver without us getting out of bed. Then we're doing the phones for the escort service and booking the girls and we're getting their eighty buck fee 24 hours a day and Rita takes the best jobs at the Hilton and the Sheraton and I'm driving her up and down Highway 101 and our pockets are crammed full of fifties and some of the tricks want half ounces of coke so I'm getting out the talcum powder and the needle doesn't have a chance to breathe it's so busy drilling holes up our arms. We got $2000 credit anytime we want and I'm taking Klonopins on top of the smack 'cos I can't feel it anymore and I'm getting sloppy and taking two hours to find a vein so when the phone rings for a job I can't be fucked to pick it up 'cos I'm busy with a thick syringe full and then Rita starts having to put pancake on her arms and her hands 'cos the track marks are shining purple and the tricks start freaking out in case she's got AIDS and we've burned all the escort services of their cut so we're blacklisted and we're being followed by Feds in unmarked cars and I start carrying weapons in case someone tries to take the syringe out of my arm and Pedro and his boys come over to get their two grand and I have to take a walk while Rita fucks them all in our bed so they won't shoot us and I don't really care anymore 'cos I'm fucking tired.

When I first walked down Mission Street aged 19 and took a

left on 24th I knew I was in enemy territory. By the time I got to Folsom all I could think was how the fuck am I gonna get out of here, I was so scared of being white and the brown eyes looking me up and down could smell it. Back then I deserved their hatred. I was a suburban middle-class gringo and my fathers had fucked them in the ass on a regular basis for generations, they still do, no it took a lot of madness and crime and violence for me to belong down there and ten years later I was a predator on the very streets I used to fear. That's what action accomplishes, burglaries, robberies, car chases, stabbings, fixing in the alleys and introducing the good Mexican fathers to the new blonde hooker who'd just hit town carved out a place for me where I belonged. I did time with their children and sold the neighbourhood the bounties from my raids into white suburbia. The scent of frijoles and the slapping hands of corn tortillas announcing another barrio morning is as close as I've come to belonging since the African idyll, there's something about poverty and oppression that breeds a natural grace, like I said I'm a sentimentalist and I just hate white cunts and it's funny now I behave myself that's what I'm becoming, just another white cunt in a long tradition.

Redwood City Jail is a shithole, it's a venereal wart sponsored by one of the richest counties in America. They start running breakfast at 3.30 in the morning, a boiled egg and two pieces of bread, the cells are so full there's bodies all over the floor, the dum dums in for domestic abuse or drunk driving think they gotta be someone, they're not, and, at first, the mentally ill are housed in general population until they get their heads caved in by some idiot wannabe. It's almost all black, Mexican or Samoan so if you're a white boy kicking smack forget it. There's no detox or medication you just ride it out lying on the floor by the toilet so you can puke and shit each time you get the strength to stand. That's where I learned how to bang my head on the wall until I bled and say I had a seizure, that's where I learned to say I had AIDS and tuberculosis so I could get into the medical tank and get some more to eat and beg meds off the crazies, thorazine librium haldol it didn't matter just give me something you cunts. But when you get your strength back hell changes, you start to make a place for yourself and get a routine, push-ups sit-ups, spades with the Mexicans you can speak Spanish so that's the crew you hang with, the few whites are neanderthals on speed and clueless but La Raza are good people and if you get in with them you're doing OK.

I'm not a big criminal, I just want my heroin and crack and I'll do anything to get it, I'll strip dead bodies of their jewellery, I'll mug rich old ladies outside the Opera House and tear the purse from their posh little arms as they scream you bastard and go into shock. If you leave your car running while you duck into the post office it's gone stupid fuck. I'm a vulture, I'll dig through the shit in garbage bags outside veterinary hospitals looking for old syringes I can trade for new ones at the needle exchange then sell the new ones to the old black dogs who sell'em on as rockets for five bucks each. I just want twenty bucks for eternity, I just want my one and one and a nickel of rock and you can all fuck off and die 'til I need more money, then I'm coming after you preferably with a smile on my face but if that doesn't work I've got a small crowbar strapped to my left shin and, hey, nobody's looking, what do you know.

One of Rita's regulars was a fat Japanese American called Gene. Gene used to be a police chief in Honolulu but he was the proverbial trick. Rita treated him like shit and the soft prick lapped it up, she'd keep him waiting two hours in the car while we searched for tiny veins on her neck then she'd send me down to him to get more money 'cos we missed that shot and she's not leaving 'til we get it right. Gene brought her a big screen TV for the motel room and he'd show up with burritos and new shoes for her pink little toes, he'd take us out for breakfast and drive us to score and he'd sit there staring at her like a puppy dog as she ignored him. Every three months Rita got a trust fund check for three grand and we'd lock the doors for three days and celebrate. Well the morning it was due old Gene had been busy 'cos I'm in a room down the hall with some Rick James wannabe crack dealer rocking up when the door comes flying down and the fucking Undercover Task Force and Parole Department come tumbling into the room pistols in hand and beat me to the ground, they just ignored slick Rick and hog-tied me and dragged me through the motel lobby and into the waiting Ford Granada and there's old Gene parked up across the street trying to sit low in his car so I won't see him, the cunt had called me in and his buddies were happy to oblige which is no big deal but the pain of being two hours away from Rita's three grand and then being snatched reverberates to this day, good one Gene, hats off you cunt.

I'm a desert boy, I blossom in the sun take out the heroin and alcohol and I rise each morning at five and write bad poetry on my prison bunk, I play pelota with the Mexicans and am told I'm pretty good for a white boy. I hang out with Roque the Indian who gives me books on prison meditation and tells me what the skins get up to in the sweat lodge they built on the upper yard, how they burn sage and sing to their ancestors and be reminded of how much they've lost, take out the whiskey and they're like wild horses with nowhere to go.

CRC State Penitentiary is close to Palm Springs, it's fucking hot and there isn't a swimming pool but there is a water main on the yard that shoots out a cold river, you bend down and put your head into its stream and soak, then you throw back your hair and let the water run down your brown skin and look up at the clear blue sky and say "I have arrived".

I did three or four terms at CRC I can't remember but my number was N62613. That's me on the yard doing pull ups and dips and sit-ups and laughing with the locos drinking black coffee and smoking buglers while listening to The Fall on my old Walkman, that's me with Tybor the mad Hungarian who can do a thousand push-ups straight and laughs about the hole in his jaw where he was shot by the cop who was fucking his wife, the cop he came after covered in blood and beat into a twelve-year sentence. Then there's Perry and Jason and Rocky the 19-year-old lost boys who tag around like I'm their bad uncle, and Smiley the lifer and Topo and Slim the Crip from South Central who cut a hole in his mattress so his bitch Mitzi can crawl underneath and stick his ass up and get fucked behind a curtain of blankets at count time, Slim's a pimp don't you know. So yes I loved CRC, but all the time I'm complaining and refusing to work and filing writs to get my N number rescinded and get a regular parole tail 'cos the N number parole is a bitch and you do a year each violation instead of six months. The N number was created in the seventies for criminal junkies and the deal was if you completed your four years of parole clean your felonies were squashed but I don't think that ever happened. We just rolled in and out getting older and tireder till the day we catch twenty years because of our priors.

Don't ya know we're gonna kill, kill your sons until they run run run run away.

Dorm 203 on the lower yard of the California Rehabilitation Center in Norco is not a bad place to be. It's mostly a mixture of N numbers doing two to six or lifers who've already served twenty and have behaved enough to edge down in categorisation. Level Two means wing living, eighty-man dorms, two big yards open 'til sundown in the summer, an outside road crew and an armed perimeter. Dorm living means no more cells, but sometimes you miss having a cell especially if you want to eat your canteen without being bothered or visit with your favourite *Hustler* magazine centrefold with some privacy, but where there's a will there's always a way. Sometimes late at night on the way to the bathroom half of the bunks in the dorm would be squeaking away, kind of rocking back and forward to that old sex beat, they'd stop as you walked by then pick up where they left off as you moved out of range.

I want to clarify something, just in case you're interested, since it seems like most people think that you got to cover your ass in prison at all times, that no matter what you look like, some troglodyte with thirty years is just waiting for you to drop the soap in the shower so when you bend over he can grab you by the hair and stick his cock up your innocent ass. That's not my experience. The fact is, in California at least, there's enough bitches to go round, by bitches I mean homosexual men who when they find themselves in an all-male arena tend to exaggerate their feminine qualities.

Take Ra Ra for example. Ra Ra's real name is Robert and he has a face like a St Bernard dog but Ra Ra can fight and he's definitely not scared. After a month Ra Ra starts cutting his boxers into panties and dyeing them pink with packets of red Kool-Aid from his bag lunches and tying his t-shirts in a bow on his chest. Ra Ra starts working out on his ass every day and it just blossoms out like a flower, thigh lifts and butt crunches and squats and scissor crosses, he lies on his stomach and raises his legs behind him and points his throat up at the sky and grabs hold of his ankles and squeezes those butt cheeks tight until they stand to attention.

Now Ra Ra's not for just anybody, oh no, Ra Ra knows who's worthy of his awesome ass and it's got to be a shot caller it's got to be a bad ass motherfucker who is surrounded by flunkies and a rep that goes back at least ten years and when the man disappears into the shower room with Ra Ra everybody just gets on with their business and smile when they come out like it's droit du seigneur, but should some nobody peckerwood have the gall to let Ra Ra suck his dick he would be in for a very bad time, fists and boots and everything he owns taken away, his locker stripped naked and him sitting on his bare mattress waiting for the cop to let him roll it up and "get the fuck out of here faggot!"

Then there's the chapel run. The chapel run seems to have developed a special dispensation because on chapel run the girls go first and jump over the walkway walls between wings into the bushes and then the fellas come down on their way to church. It's night time and dark and out of a group of thirty, ten end up in the service while the rest are in the bushes getting their dicks sucked and pulling down Kool-Aid panties and coming over the open mouths ringed with five o'clock shadow until they wait for chapel recall and jump over the wall and fall into line with their homeys and it's like nothing ever happened, but only on a Sunday, amen brother.

Steve was a nobody kid doing a little two year first-timer welcome pack, he was a local boy with silky smooth black hair parted on the left and soft olive skin and that's how it started. Steve is trying to make friends and be one of the guys when he lets drop that his sister lives in the neighbourhood and she can bring him speed into visits and would any one like some?

Smiley is a lifer, he's done 23 already for a double murder in the seventies and he's kind of immaculate he is pure chicano cholo with a Zapata moustache and he irons his jeans with two creases down the middle of the front and combs his black hair straight back with a palm brush and wears State-issue clothes but only the best. Smiley is a panther and the next thing you know is that Steve is bringing Smiley balloons of speed every Saturday after visits, he's swallowing little gram balloons his sister spits into her coffee cup, which is all well and good but as you'd expect Smiley says "quarter ounce next time kid OK?". "OK" says Steve 'cos he's feeling popular now. The next Saturday and everyone's waiting for Stevie to return and go into the bathroom which he does but something's gone wrong he's in there a long time. So Smiley goes over to see what happening and Stevie can't bring it up he's swallowed a quarter ounce of speed wrapped in plastic and it's stuck in his stomach and it's not budging. Smiley gave him all sorts of liquids to help him puke his package up but it's not working, Smiley even holds him by the hair and sticks four fingers down his throat and rams them in and out but it's no good he's just bringing up blood and green shit and now he's getting scared and Smiley says relax homes you can shit it out tomorrow.

Tomorrow comes and it doesn't look good for Steve 'cos he's started twitching and jerking and rolling his jaw in a circle when he tries to speak and he can't get the words out he just goes uurrrguuaaaa uuuurrrrrgggguuuuu and Smiley says fuck the fucking package has split open inside him, so now we're all watching Steve. For three days this kid flops around the floor of the dorm twitching and jerking and going uuurraaaaauuuuuaaah how the cops didn't notice before they did

I don't know. Steve tries to play cards every now and then or bounces along the hallway going to chow but it's no use he's fucking poisoned. Steve's swallowed all this speed and he's lost it and now his little cock is standing straight up through his boxers 24/7 and I think that every time he brushed it with his hand he was cumming he just oozed this crazy fuck me smell and Smiley would raise his nose in the air and twitch his nostrils and that would be it. Smiley moved his bunky out and set up a curtain, a ring of State-issue grey blankets around his bunk, and he'd take little Steve by the hand and lead him into his tent and you could just hear these gurgles and wet sounds coming out like the plumbing was exploding and then Stevie would crawl out and do circles around the floor on his hands and knees like he was a cockroach and then Smiley would appear and lead him into the shower and wash him down and tell him to shut up.

Three days later the cops took him out. Maybe some good citizen had had enough and dropped a note under the door, who knows, but we'd all had enough of the little honeymoon Smiley had taken. Order was restored which is always a good thing, until you get bored that is. So yea, 203 isn't a bad place, in fact some people have been here a long time and are running a tight program.

Little Bob lived on the bottom at the first bunk by the cop shop. When you first saw him you'd think what the fuck is he doing here? He was barely five foot tall and round like a bowling ball with these thick bottle-neck glasses over his little brown owl eyes, he'd look at you and blink ten times before he could figure out what to say. He wore his blue jeans high over his waist way up on his belly with that rope belt you see on the robes of Franciscans or the brotherhood of catamites and that was what Bob was, the high priest of the catamites, but we didn't know for sure until they tried to release him and 500 angry mothers and fathers showed up at the prison gates with placards and photos of the children he'd got hold of with their faces blacked out. Little Bob wore those Christian sandals with grey socks and a big plastic crucifix hung from his neck on a piece of shoelace. Bob used to have Bible study on his bunk for the youngsters in the wing, he'd bake a cake in the chapel kitchen and get Kool-Aid and cookies and open up his big Mormon Bible to page 307 and they'd take turns reading a sentence and then talk about what it meant to them. Bob had been down a long time, he'd been down so long and in so many different prisons that nobody knew who he was any more. Little Edgar was his altar boy, little Edgar was a skinny Filipino kid from Bakersfield about 19 or 20 he was kind of like the wing's puppy dog, his front teeth were knocked out and he tried to walk like a gangster and claimed sureño and was covered in bad YA ink but he was just a Saturday morning cartoon. Little Edgar would wash your boxers and socks for a cigarette and he'd make your bunk for a cup of coffee and every time he spoke he had to laugh 'cos it always seemed like it was the funniest thing in the world. So Bob and Edgar hold services for all the new youngsters who come in and at first they get a bunk full 'til the fish figure out that Bob's bunk is definitely not a good place to be seen on a regular basis, then it's thin pickings until the next fresh face shows up, and lucky for Bob they always did.

Bob turned out to be one of the first guys to volunteer to have his balls cut off as a condition of his parole, and now he's probably padding around some high security motel with his Bible in his fat little fingers because really he's never getting out, just like Smiley, but the difference is that Smiley would probably die before he let them cut of his balls. Smiley had a Bible he used to read on Sundays and he had a plastic rosary with a little crucifix hanging off the bottom and he had a big tattoo of the Virgin of Guadeloupe across his perfect chest. That's what I learned in Dorm 203, but all of that stuff is just window dressing on the surface, like Little Red Riding Hood and the Big Bad Wolf, you never really know who's sleeping in the bunk next to you not 'til after the fact, and for all Bob's little cherubs who must have wondered what kind of Bible study that had been, and for Steve with that big bag of speed leaking into his guts and Smiley's cock up his ass, that was just a little too late.

In my last term at San Quentin I started writing to prisoners abroad, I wanted to escape the carnage that was my life and like most people I thought a change of scenery would do the trick. I hadn't been to London since 1981 and when I found out I had an immigration hold I found myself lying in my west block cell pretending to be humble, no I wouldn't use or rob or steal, I would get a job cleaning the toilets in Piccadilly Circus and listen to BBC Radio 4 on a small transistor radio and I'd be grateful and quiet kind of like a Benedictine monk of the urinals, but as my release date got closer and closer and no immigration showed up for me the adrenalin of my reality crept back. I don't know how many county jail terms I served but I'd done four state prison terms before this one and every time parole day comes along this crazy euphoria gets hold of me and bang I'm gone from the gate. No parole officers ever met me unless they kicked down a motel door or came to get a statement after I'd been arrested again on some new charge. When those prison doors open and they hand you $200 in an envelope it's a race to 16th and Mission, "mi barrio", it's a heart-thumping sprint 300 miles to Rita's crack pipe and that first real shot that's haunted my sleep since the cuffs went on.

"Hey man, hey you CRC, don't you remember me?" He was small and hard like a wild goat with bitter blue eyes and long dirty blonde hair. He was holding the bars of the bullpen across the walkway. "It's Jeff," he said, "Jeff from Chico, we done time down in Norco don't you remember?" I looked up from the bench in the transportation cell and thought for a while, Then it came, the white's card room in 302 about 16 months ago he'd been playing pinochle with Cody from Davis and they got into a fight, Cody had beat him from one end of the card room to the other, he'd bounced his head off all the walls and broken his ribs and the little goat had crawled out the door and Cody sat back down and finished his hand and then the goat came flying back through the door with a shank cut out of a tin can with string wrapped around for a handle and the goat had stuck Cody three times in his back and punctured his lung and Cody had just stood back up and kicked his ass again.

"Oh yea," I said, "I remember."

"Yea," said the goat nodding his head and trying to smile. "Man, it's been fucked up since then."

"Yea? What did they do with you?"

"Fuck man I spent a year in the hole at Chino and I been on transportation for four fucking months since then, they lost all my property and I been driving in circles around California living on choke sandwiches and sleeping on the floors of every fucking county jail in the state."

"That's not good", I said, thinking how much I truly didn't care.

And the goat shook his head and just for a moment I thought the goat was gonna cry but he looked back down at the ground and said, "You don't got a smoke do you?"

"Yea", I said and put my hands, which were shackled together, up to my left ear and plucked out a roll up and tossed it through the bars onto the concrete walkway.

"Thanks man."

"OK", I said and stared back at the floor and hoped that the conversation had come to an end.

It was 4 a.m. and the pens were full and this was R and R, reception and release not rest and recreation. The first two pens were full of inmates paroling and the rest of the pens were waiting on transportation. I had an immigration hold whatever that meant nobody told you anything down here. That's just how it was. They put me in a dayglo orange paper jump suit and shackled my ankles and taken my Converse and put me in a State-issue pair of jap flaps. The chain ran up to my waist and wrapped around the outside of the suit then down and around my wrists. You had to shuffle your feet in eight-inch steps to move. Now what you did was pray, pray that they would fuck up and call your name for parole, that they would get it wrong and undo the chains and hand you some dress outs and open the gates. It had happened before, they'd let me out of San Francisco county at two in the morning when I was waiting to be sentenced on a parole violation. One minute you're doing two years and the next you're walking down Bryant Street in the beautiful rain with a snake rolling round in your stomach demanding to be fed.

Sixteen hours later and it was standing room only, Cubans and Vietnamese and fuck knows what else all speaking in broken English trying to figure out where they were being sent too, the Mexicans were jammed in the pen across the way they were all going back to Tijuana then they'd swim back across the river the following night.

Now you just prayed to be fed. When you're hungry that's good enough. The goat was long gone.

At midnight they opened the pen door and lined us up on the black tar outside in a white painted square. We all got given a paper bag with our property inside and our number written across the face in black ink. Then they told us to squat down and shut up.

The bus rumbled out of the side gate big and grey with blacked-out windows covered in steel bars, the grey goose

CDC transportation. It had its own separate army of guards in black jumpsuits and jackboots, shotguns and pistol holsters worn high on the leather belt that circled the waist, moustaches and mirrored shades at midnight. The sergeant stood up front by the door to the bus and looked down at the clipboard in his hands, he had a toothpick in his mouth, he looked up spat out the toothpick and stepped forward:

"Rule number one no talking. Rule number two no fucking talking or we bounce your heads off of every piece of metal in my bus. Rule number three, look straight ahead not at the scum bag on your left or your right any problems and I lock you in the idiot box and we lose all your property and we kick your ass any time we feel like it understood?"

There was no response.

"Good. Now when I call your number step up to the bus drop your bag on the ground and wait for the officer to signal that you can board, two at a time right. Two go in, the next two wait, just like Noah's Ark, got it?"

No response.

"Good. Let's do it."

"N62613, H5187, step up."

We crossed the Golden Gate Bridge as the sun was coming up in the east. Folsom, Soledad, Vacaville, CRC lunch bag. We spent the night in Modesto County Jail. I had half a can of Bugler wrapped in plastic up my ass but I couldn't get to the county inmates who'd pay five dollars for a pin-sized roll up so I just pulled it out and rolled up twenty and handed them around to the amigos then stuck it back inside. At 6 a.m. we were back on board with blisters on our ankles and wrists.

The Party, 2011
110 × 160 cm

The Last Motel, 2006
133 × 160 cm

Silesia, 2009
111 × 154 cm

Gilles de Rais, 2011
96 × 125 cm

Highway 5 goes on forever, I've hitched it too many times. It's butt ugly and I'd always been in a hurry to get the fuck on but I just knew how good it would be to be stuck out here on an on ramp today with my thumb in the air and a semi heading to Santa Barbara pulling up for you to climb into.

By Paso Robles I thought if you pressed your face right on the black glass window the girls in the cars driving next to the bus might just be able to see how handsome you were and you could stick out your tongue and pretend you were eating their pussy and they'd get the creeps and step on the gas and then turn around and wave as they pulled away. By the time we got to Avenal the cops had let up through boredom and most people were talking away in low whispers. I'd been sat next to a fat Chinaman since Soledad and hadn't even bothered with more than a glance. It was hot, they handed out some water in plastic jugs every four hours. To piss or shit you had to raise your hands for the gunner who rode high in a sealed off perch of bulletproof glass in the back to nod you down, he had a shotgun laid across his lap. After Delano I started thinking how a prison bus is like a ghost ship sailing down the freeway, other cars get out of the way or ride your side for a moment to grab a look and wonder who the fuck is in there and what they did, you can feel the attention and part of you starts to believe that you're part of a mad Viking horde heading to Valhalla instead of petty little pieces of shit thinking of how to get twenty dollars sent in quick from your mother.

So the fat Chinaman's from Vietnam and he's finished his five years for conspiracy to supply and now he's heading to a federal penitentiary forever perhaps, because there's no official agreement between America and Vietnam on the deportation of prisoners, the same with the Russians and the Cubans. He is not happy. He says he's been in the states since he was three years old and is a college graduate for Christ sakes! Then the gunner opens his eyes and yells shut the fuck up.

As we pulled up to LA County Jail I had a sinking feeling in my stomach. I was in a minority of one, white boy, blue eyes, blonde hair and LA County was famous for being a little bit dark, black as the night sky you might say, except for the sureños but they rode with the brothers down here not like the norteños I'd left in Quentin who were supposed to ride with the whites but that was all bullshit anyway because you know it was better just to ride it alone.

At LA County they put us on the floor of some sad ass hallway, took off our chains and locked the doors. We'd missed dinner and nobody gave a fuck but us. In the morning they lined us up and chained our sorry asses again and started the same fucking speech all over. I was tired, this was day number three riding this hell tank like a pinball bouncing all over California, now nobody cared what the gunner had to say and the idiot box looked like a break in the monotony of being a well behaved cow en route to the butchers.

By Barstow we could tell that we were in a convoy, another grey goose pulled up on the left and the drivers honked at each other and the inmates pounded their shackled hands on the windows to say hello but it was just black glass and bars. When we crossed the state line into Nevada we were empty heads bouncing on top of stinking bodies and I thought about the goat in the holding cell back at Quentin how he'd been on this ride for four months all because he was an asshole and even the cops didn't like him and I remembered stories of convicts doing a year lost in transportation and how the Feds had 51 states to chain you up and drive you around if they so desired, they could even fly you to Alaska or Hawaii locked up in the idiot box with the shackles cutting into your hips and your wrists and your ankles and you couldn't even have a smoke cause they were always there watching you through their mirrored shades with a shotgun on their lap and a toothpick in their mouth just like the movies. By the time we hit Arizona I said it out loud looking straight at the gunner, "it's all just like the movies" and I felt just a little bit better.

Hello you mother fuckers are you still here? OK.

Back in '98 Eloy federal pen was one of the first privatised prisons to be running, so that meant it was a flagship for investors and senators and the toothless community activists to all come along and see how wonderful it was all gonna be. Look, our fat happy convicts even eat meals with the guards.
    "Gee Mr Convict could you pass the tortillas and salsa."
    "Sure thing Mr Guard."
    "Thank you very much Mr Convict."
    "Oh don't mention it, my pleasure."
    But Eloy had a big ass wing out back, the AAC, that's the Attitude Adjustment Center to you, where they were full to the brim with convicts who just couldn't stomach the kinder, softer way, no, they preferred to go out banging their heads on the blacked-out walls of their cells rather than eat with the

warden and his pretty little secretary. Some of these guys had been down twenty years in the finest shitholes America has to offer, Marielitos from the prisons of Cuba via Leavenworth and fuck knows where else, add to that the inconvenient fact that they'd already done their time and now found themselves locked up anyway, yes we know we said twenty years but that was just the courts, you're dealing with us now and you ain't going nowhere Pedro.

"So who the fuck are you?"

"Homeland Security you wetback motherfucker."

Yea yea yea who cares? I'm not banging my head on anything any more, I'm going back to London.

So Ignacio gets rolled up at 5 a.m. and he's giving me a big bear hug smiling ear to ear 'cos he's forgotten for a moment that he's probably gonna get shot in 24 hours.

"Mi hermano, mi hermano" he's saying.

And I'm saying "si si amigo yo voy viva the Basques!" Save me a spot on the beach and a fat syringe full.

And then he's gone.

I'm at the airport in Phoenix, Arizona, I'm wearing State-issue blue jeans, a white t-shirt and a pair of stinking Converse on my feet that I was arrested in, god knows when, that's all that's in my property bag, a pair of crack foot sneakers and a book I must have had tucked in the back of my belt when I got done, Evelyn Underhill's *The Mystical Experience*, I got handcuffs on and I'm holding the book like a Bible in my cuffed hands trying to figure out why the fuck I would have been carrying this book around the underbelly of the Mission and I'm standing in between two federal transportation guards at the entrance gate to British Airways flight 101 to Gatwick. The boarding staff are looking at me in horror 'cos the cops seem to think it's a good idea to stand me there facing all the nice passengers as they boarded the plane because I got to go on last. So I'm smiling at the nice people as they go by to get on the plane but part of me is tired of this game, tired of being paraded in public with manacles and chains like I'm on the way to the village stocks to get pelted with rotten tomatoes and dog shit. The last passenger has boarded and the chief steward is standing there getting handed my temporary passport and my deportation orders for the authorities in London and the Feds uncuff my hands and take the chains off my waist and uncuff my ankles and I smile at the steward 'cos really I'm a nice guy, and he smiles back and walks me on to the plane and gives me a front row seat right next to the cabin crew and I smile to the old lady next to me and the business man next to her and I sit in my seat with my head back on the rest and take a deep breath and close my eyes.

I'm free, there's this kind of bright clean feeling running up and down my veins and the air tastes different as I breathe in and out slowly and calmly and the engines roar and we head down the tarmac and I'm swearing to myself (again) this is it I'm a changed man no more drugs no more prison no more robbing or lying or… Fuck as the plane climbs into the air something terrible is happening inside my skull, my head is exploding, all my cracked teeth and my shattered jaw bones are just screaming in agony as the pressure mounts up as we rise, tears come down my face and as we level out I raise my hands in desperation to get the stewardess's attention. "Yes, may I help you" she says.

"Double brandy and a beer back, please" I say. So much for sobriety I need some fucking medication.

London was a gift, at first, like a gentle hospice in the netherworld where you just drink methadone and eat a big fry-up in the hostel canteen, in England they gave you money each week so if you were half broken like me you didn't really do any more crime, you just waited outside Boots at ten to eight each morning and on benefit day you stroll down to Brixton to pick up a sixteenth of crack, the heroin was so shit and cut to hell and if you had a script of 120 like mine it hardly touched you any way, no, you drink cheap cider and have a craic with the old alkies who give you dosh to get their cans and are too drunk to remember you owe them change. I'd never been so broken as when I gave up the criminal ghost and flatlined it for two and a half years, 87 men stuck in sheol, 87 ghosts standing at the threshold of being and not being. The body bags crept out quietly and we'd have a drink to old Nick or Tommy or Marco the crazy Italian or whoever it was that day heading to the crematorium at Kensal Green. Some days I'd sleep for 18 hours my bed covered in books about poltergeists and translocation and the mystic weeping of stone statues, my light was always on so when I came to I'd read another page then drift away again and again and again.

Kiwi Kev was a Kiwi, hey what do you know, he had a script for six injectable amps per day lucky cunt. On bank holidays that's 18 amps all worth ten to 15 quid each. Kev was my mate, everyone liked Kev, even the hostel staff, we'd come back from Boots and I'd hit him up and off to Tottenham Court Road in the alleys off Soho Square where junkies went to buy amps. A hundred quid later and we're in Shepherds Bush 'cos Kevin's always got good Yardie contacts for eightballs of crack then the mad dash back to the hostel with some citric flying up the stairs to his room where we'd pull out a big spoon and drop a fat rock into the citric and cook it up post haste. I'd have to hit him first before I got mine, Kev's been shooting for twenty years and can't stand the sight of his own blood, which for me is fantastic 'cos my services are required. Kev closes his eyes and rolls up his pant leg and I go to work, the thing is I got to be quick 'cos once Kev gets his shot he loses it completely, for some people shooting cocaine releases all the demons from hell and the terror they have paid for is a wonder to behold. I hit him just above the ankle and grab my syringe. As I'm trying to find a vein I see Kev is losing the battle, the demons are taking hold and he drops to his knees staring beneath the crack of the door in terror, he starts hyperventilating and waving his arm to me "who's there?" he says "who's there?" He jumps up doing figure eights with his tongue now he can't speak just gesticulates that he needs to search me in case I'm wired up with a police mic, I let him pat me down and turn out my pockets as I try to push the plunger down 'cos I just saw a red trickle in the barrel, but then Kev starts screaming and tearing off his clothes and I gotta be quick 'cos it's the same routine he'll run into the hallway and cower on the stairs calling for James his key worker and I need to be back in my room with my piece of rock 'cos I've got business to take care of. Kev set his room on fire one morning, turned over his mattress emptied out all of his drawers in a big pile and set it on flames. They had to kick him out and I was truly sorry to see him go. Kev was my mate. Good oh Kev, cheers buckaroo.

Calling Sister Midnight I'm a breakage inside
Calling Sister Midnight what can I do about my dreams?

I'm dying slowly in bed, drowning in methadone linctus, olanzapine, diazepam and cheap cider, early in the mornings something crawls out from behind the hostel curtains and slithers over to sit on top of my chest, it pins me down and sucks the air out from my lungs and puts my balls in its mouth and bites down like an old man in the gas chambers of Treblinka taking his last breath.
    Guilty.
    Guilty.
    Guilty as charged.

Guess what?
    What?
    Heroin bores me, I've had enough, after 25 years all I can hear is the clink of the lighter as it falls to the floor, I pick it up and then clink, it drops again, I pick it up and clink clink clink, that bell's tolling for you, tolling over an eternity of nothingness a flatline nirvana with just your abscesses and you to

contemplate no one's left to bother you now just 100 empty bottles of methadone and the Sharps containers you took out of the hostel toilets hoping to find someone else's clogged syringe and the coloured girls go do de do de do de do. So what do you do now? You're 42 years old, haven't worked a day since you were 18. It's 2003 and you've never used a computer or owned a mobile phone, like Kasper Hauser you just walk into town out of the forest and sit in the square a note pinned to your jacket with the dumb innocence of childhood as your only saving grace.

I'm so quick to say I don't give a fuck when really I do, I give a big fuck about everything I just didn't know where to start.

Sex is a commodity, we buy it, sell it, trade it, withdraw it from the market to raise its value for a while then bring it back when the timing seems right. Sex is a weapon we use it to inflict punishment on those we accuse, it can be whipped out like a knife to even the score or used as a tool in the sacrifice of self-destruction and ruin. And sometimes sex can save your life.

She called herself Jazz but really her name was Jennifer. She was a natty dread pixie from Blackpool who wore six-inch platform boots and stomped around like a bomb explosion all five foot one of her, she had a tight little body, amazing tits and she was my key worker. When I was referred from Prisoners Abroad she took me in the back office and did the interview. Now I love a good interview with a caring professional, especially if they look like Jennifer and for two hours she winced and laughed and even shed a tear as I went through my routine, now you're talking to a guy whose last sex was a business proposition with a queen in San Bruno County Jail, I let him give me a blow job in the shower in exchange for his lunch cookies for a week, top class stuff eh? Oh yea I was dope sick and hungry but there's always an excuse, anyway when the interview was over I knew we were meant to be, she knew it too, only she was in love with Steff, a charming old junky gone straight and working in a hostel in Soho. He used to come in to pick her up and she'd scream like a child and jump into his arms wrapping her legs around him and leaning back, all the hostel lads playing pool would pause for the performance and I would slink off to my room. I liked Jennifer so much that I refused to speak to her and punished her every chance I could get, this was an old routine, the sulking little prince, the self-pitying 40-year-old child, how sweet. Stroppy cunt.

When you've slipped beneath the borders of society you know it and so do they. Sometimes you can use this as a weapon as you bowl down the street but if someone shines a light in your eyes you're caught like a cockroach on the kitchen floor, you are the untouchable the unlovable and the unredeemable you're gone you're broken you're headed for the glue factory with "surplus requirement" stamped on your ass. Most of us oblige and die quietly, in the park under the proverbial bridge or outside the hospital having our last cigarette in a wheelchair after scuttling through the lobby with our mobile IV antibiotics stand rattling in one hand. We don't even merit a sigh unless you count the huff from the paramedic as he zips another body bag. No, it's the way of the world, the broken gotta go nothing personal but we sure as fuck aren't all in this together we're in this alone and when you realize this you just might have a chance.

December of 2001 James calls me down to reception and says I have an appointment to view a flat in Holland Park. This is good, there's money on the horizon, everyone in the hostel sits on their ass watching Star Trek waiting for the proverbial flat as if your gonna be beamed up to another planet where everything's gonna be perfect. Ha, you're still you, stupid fuck, you're still the same cunt who gets his meals cooked and his dishes washed and the staff even help you do your laundry 'cos you've started to smell bad again so anyway off I trot with Geordie Pete to sign the contract and get my £1650 for heroin and crack, oops I mean ovens and fridges and drapery, yea right. Three days later I wake up broke in this tiny box on my own, no cooked breakfast, no free Klix coffee vending machine, no one to go in halves on a cider never mind a rock just little old me and the nice neighbours who watch me through the peepholes in their doors. I realized the disaster of what I'd done no more Football Italia with the boys on Sunday morning no more Sharps bins in the toilets to raid for clogged syringes no more pool competitions or quizzes to win a week's dinner tickets no more fat ash trays to pilfer for the never ending roll up. I think I almost cried.

Knock knock. "Who's there?"

"Jennifer"

"Jennifer who?"

"It's Jazz you silly cunt open the door."

So here she is two and a half years late standing outside my front door with a bottle of red wine in her hand, girls aren't they the best? The love of her life has gone from counsellor to rehab resident in a heartbeat 'cos he picked up the smacky-poo again and she was waking up to find syringes under her pillow and blood all over the toilet walls, that's part of the excitement of being around recovering addicts, their realities can flip at the drop of a coin. Anyway she's kicked him out and ping! remembered that handsome old cad she used to watch on the office CCTV doing push-ups in the poolroom on methadone and coffee, she goes through the resident aftercare records when no one's around and writes down my new address.

"Fuck, it looks like Miss Havisham's in here! Come on open this bottle and let's go."

Off we trot to the Elgin on Ladbroke Grove and play pool and she buys us drinks and starts telling me how she kept all the poems I wrote (I don't remember any poems) and how all the staff used to say what a shame Chris is so fucked up 'cos there's something special about him, (now you're talking, that's better) and how sometimes on roomcheck she used to want to stay behind and find out what I was made of and enough already she's leaning across the pool table trying to make the most of taking a shot and showing me how sweet her little ass is and I go over and give her a big wet kiss and that's it she's practically fucking me in every doorway to her house and she's hot and smells like cinnamon and her skin is velvet like a horse's muzzle and it's been so fucking long I can't even remember who I am anymore.

So I wake up next morning with tank girl curled up next to me and Iggy the black Battersea terrier snoring away in his little basket and I think this is different, this is kinda nice compared to the cobwebs and empty cider bottles I was used to, and suddenly I'm not in any hurry to get to Boots to pick up my methadone in fact I run to Holland Park and start to do my rehab Tai Chi and push-ups and sit-ups and I write Jennifer's name in flowers and leave it in the bird bath near the bicycle path she rides down on her way to work and I call up the crisis team and set up my 99th detox and I think about the book I'm gonna write and suddenly remember my granddad Jimmie Turnbull died two years ago and out of nowhere I feel like crying and the trees are watching me with their beautiful indifference.

Why don't you write about smell? You never really mention it, people need to be engaged by the representation of all their senses. Perhaps start with an abscess, that mixture of ammonia and ass juice that's leaking out of your wrist, the dead mouse that you swallowed that's been reincarnated as the puss you wipe on your trouser leg, or the stink of burning plastic and dying old men that came out of Melanie's pussy the first time you fingered her and she laughed as you gagged and said oh honey that's just a staph infection from your dad sticking his fat cock in my cunt after he's fucked me in the ass.

Or the pink sweet vomit of industrial cleaner rising from the cinema's basement steps in Soho, the trigger that makes you wretch 'cos it tastes just like a big shot of crack or the angel song of horse shit that comes out of the corral on the Scrubs that smells like god just might exist, if you pay attention.

William was the crown prince of junkies, he was elegant and devastated at the same time. I first saw him in the garden at our Clapham Common rehab drinking a cup of chai in a floral print kimono, his long hair up in a samurai bun, old abscesses up and down his arms and legs. William was an aristocratic runaway street kid, he had the residue of "London Punks" in a child's handwriting tattooed on his neck and he spoke like the ghost of Lord Byron. William was my roommate and he was a filthy pig, I loved him, I brought him his coffee in bed each morning and kicked his clothes over to his side of the room before waking him up for another day of "therapeutic recovery".

William was an artist but all he did was shoot heroin and smoke crack and sell it to the fallen sons and daughters of the aristocracy, the damaged little heirlings who break apart to punish mummy and daddy, the one's who can smoke a trust fund in six months and spend the rest of their lives on methadone with a posh accent lurking like ravens at the family Christmas for some crumbs to bring to William, posh beggars, don't you love them. Anyway William was an artist and that's how it all started. William got the staff to give us a small room twice a week where he set up a painting studio, lining paper, kids' watercolours in plastic bottles pencils and sponges. Tony the counsellor acted as facilitator and after leaving us alone for an hour he'd come back in and we'd sit around and laugh at each others paintings, but William didn't laugh he was gentle and serious and he always noticed things we had missed, and you know what, from the beginning my shit stood out.

So what the fuck is an artist? In the pen you thought it was obvious, guys like Smiley from Pomona or Brandon the skinhead from Chico, guys who could take a wallet photo of your girl and then wham there she was in a pencil portrait looking like a sexy Virgin Mary. Artists were the tattooists who could break down a cassette Walkman, tie on a high E guitar string to the spindle, rig up a double D battery pack, a broken pen and a compass and hey presto! you got a tattoo gun, then they'd melt black chess pieces in an old Bugler can, add some toothpaste and water and the ink is ready. In the pen they call it ink fever, some guys get obsessed and gotta have their whole body covered in their claimed history. Tattoos in the pen can get you killed. The sureños' sworn duty is to kill norteños and the bulldogs gotta watch out for both. The first thing you hear in the holding pen is "Where you from Homey?" and you think thank god you're not a chicano. I'm a little old-fashioned and think art is something that can have repercussions, or is a testament to lived experience or a plea to the gods, the Virgin is everywhere in the pen, she's across 100,000 brown backs her eyes raised to the heavens both hands open to receive a blessing or a sentence so I guess I can forgive myself for taking this shit seriously.

The first book I remember reading that hit me hard was

something I found under my father's pillow when I was about eight, we were staying on this island in the Indian Ocean with some friends of the family, Pemba, Pemba, Pemba, and they had this little girl with blonde curly hair and sky blue eyes who kept running up to me and lifting up her dress and showing me her tiny pussy, then she'd laugh all crazy and run away again, anyhow I found this book under daddy's pillow and opened it up and started reading about some lady who was lying naked with her hands tied behind her back on an orange carpet, and she's asking this man to burn her on her ass with a lit cigarette, please, she was saying but he didn't really want to but she kept saying please, please. So he did.

This for me was the birth of poetry, the kick in the gut, the soft cry of the horse that they shot in the head that morning in the corral after it had broken its leg, riding you out at midnight to the Indian mounds with Sydney Lee Rhodes naked and drunk holding on tight to your waist, going faster and faster, the sound of the immaculate old man from Buenos Aires who keeps calling you mummy as you fuck him in his tired old saggy ass just before you rob him, he knows you're going to rob him, he's dying for you to rob him and kick him in the stomach on your way out the door because he's writing his own poem and you're just a character that he requires to articulate his special little song.

Right?
Right?
Right?

Ah, how sweet, the little prick started painting and it's happy ever after, no, get fucked, remember the ballad of Jack Henry Abbott the part-time lifer who started writing to Norman Mailer from his cell? Mailer published their letters and all Manhattan claimed Abbott as a genius. They all testify at his parole hearing and he's released with a big book contract and two weeks later stabs some guy to death at a restaurant 'cos he wouldn't let him use the toilet.

I'm not here for salvation, I'm here to get my power back.

I'm clean now, five months' worth, I'm clean but I'm fucking crazy. At my first aftercare group after being discharged from Thurston House I start talking about how I want to play Russian Roulette and Tony the counsellor, who I love, ignores me and starts asking someone else in the group to speak, I lose it, I rise from my chair and explain I'm not fucking joking then proceed to punch out all the windows in reach, I'm punching and kicking and saying I'm not fucking joking and my arm starts to spray paint the room as I've severed arteries and sliced through my meridian nerve and Tony can tell I'm not fucking joking and my head starts spinning as I try to walk out the room and Frank's wrapping towels around my arm and William's saying oh sweetie and I start to shake and go into shock but I don't know that, I'm listening to the helicopters again, flying in low over the horizon just like in *Jacob's Ladder* just like a cocaine seizure and everything shifts and I'm back in the Indian fields and I'm 11 years old and the universe kisses my cheek and then I'm in the ambulance with William's face over me saying oh sweetie oh sweetie just like he should be my mum and everything's alright 'cos here comes the morphine.

PHOTOGRAPH:
Polaroid, bleached sepia.
Interior of a liquor store.

In the aisle, three figures, in the background a young boy stands staring at the lens, he is smiling, in front of him and to the left a woman in a yellow top and a short blue denim skirt is standing on the toes of her left foot and reaching her hand up to a bottle of whiskey on the top shelf, her right leg is held out behind her and extends into the air. Foreground beneath her is the back of a man without any legs perched upon a wooden board under which wheels are attached, he's leaning forward and seems to be looking up into the woman's exposed crutch.

Come on folks let's sing that recovery song:
"Twelve steps to heaven a guaranteed path to redemption, AA, NA, CA, Uncle Bob and Bill W, service and helping the still-suffering addict, come on join the community, that's doing something for itself, be part of god's chosen few he must have a plan for you if you're still alive just follow these steps and you'll see salvation in this lifetime and if you don't do exactly as we tell you you'll die you'll die you'll die amen."

I've done three good things for myself in my life, getting clean, going to NA and getting the fuck out of it. It doesn't make sense but it's true, one day's salvation is tomorrow's life sentence, you just gotta get your timing right and live to tell the tale.

I was a good soldier, a good soldier, for seven years I make tea, I put out the chairs and stay behind to wash up the cups I go to detoxes and prisons to share my experience, strength and hope I do steps one to twelve then start back again I do everything that's suggested in the literature and then some so you can't fuck with me jack and I'm getting lots of pussy and painting like a demon and waking up at 4 a.m. to do some white magic in the hallway standing on my head but at the same time I know something's wrong, I can't stand hearing my own voice any more in the fellowship rooms, and when some fucker with ten years clean takes an hour to tell his sorry little tale I'm bouncing my feet and digging my fingernails into my palms with all this energy I got, I'm fucking trapped in this petty ass world of powerlessness and confessionals and dumb celebrities, and at first I think my problem is with recovery then I realise it's not. My problem is with contemporary civilization of which these people in the rooms are just a shadow. And then the penny drops, hey dumbfuck, you don't have to use to get the fuck away from Uncle Bill, you don't have to put a needle in your arm to declare your discontent with what you perceive to be your sorry lot, what's needed is some discipline and focus to help articulate the strength, courage and passion that gets you up at 4 a.m. for another day's adventures.

So I'm gonna be a garbage man I've got experience I don't have a problem with dirt and shit I'm strong and I get up early and you know people will always have trash that needs to be collected and you don't have to play the game too much just show up and get busy, so I'm gonna be an actor 'cos I'm doing improv at a theatre in North London and the lady tells me I'm good and all I do is pretend to be me and I give her a charcoal I did of Anne Frank hiding in the cupboard and she loves it and commissions me to paint a flying fish and gives me £500 and calls me each morning to listen to the poetry I wrote at 4 a.m. and takes me to the ballet and introduces me to all of her theatre pals and just wants to lean into my arms as she waits for her bus like it was fifty years ago in Ireland and suddenly she's 12 years old again and bless you lady, I'm sorry, so I'm gonna be a photographer like my buddy Gareth who used to be a junky but now he's flying all over the world for the *New York Times* and he's got books and a gallery and exhibitions in Tokyo and Stockholm and he takes pictures of me and my tattoos doing push ups in my mad hovel and now I'm on the gallery walls and I'm so stupid I think it's me but it's not it's just Gareth but he's introduced me to Larry Clark's *Tulsa* and I can see where I came from, I can see all my mad pals in these pictures with shotguns and hookers and syringes and I'm gonna make movies and talk about the freedom in degradation and runaway children and the wounds that make us choose which road to hitchhike down and how sometimes the greatest art is as simple as the destruction of promise that's why I got RUIN tattooed on my chest and it starts to make sense, at least to me.

"So why don't you talk about your mother?"

"What's there to say?"

"Well you just spent thirty years running round like a rat with rabies, where did the infection come from?"

"I was born with it."

"So now what? You're clean and crime-free. Who gives a fuck? You have to do better than that. What are you trying to say? In fact I don't even get a sense of you in these pages, you hide behind mayhem and second-hand philosophy. There's nothing there to take hold of. I think you really need to question your smugness and try to find a legitimate voice. Aren't you ashamed?"

"No. I'm blessed."

"Well, I think you suffer from delusions and hypomania and I want you to consider taking olanzapine for a while to see if your symptoms can be brought under control."

"Well, I think you suffer from the delusion of all those degrees on your wall and the only time you're you is when you're cheating on your wife, and in fact I think you need a twenty-year heroin habit to round off your education and when it's over and if you're still alive perhaps we can have a chat. Ha Ha Ha."

"So what do you think about now when you've run out of bullshit?"

I think about the Indian fields and 10-year-old Ruthie Lebis who used to come down to our fort and play spin the bottle with us boys. She'd spin and whoever it landed on got to spend ten minutes with Ruthie in the fort while the others waited their turn outside, and when it was my turn and I put my hands up her skirt and asked her not to do this with anyone else but me and she laughed and said when her father came home on weekends he put her in his bed and then she squirted the chewing gum from her mouth into mine and said time's up. And I think about Michele from Tarreytown Street whose brother would bring her over to Paul Douglas's house and we'd give him a cigarette and put a paper bag over Michele's face 'cos she was ugly and Jeff and Joe Acosta fucked her and I stood in the corner thinking something was wrong but didn't have the strength to open my mouth. And of Regina and Dia who met a doctor from Marin County at 13 and got pregnant and sold him their babies for $500 each and Deleslin from Santa Cruz who at 14 swallowed a bottle of industrial ant killer and now her stomach was all plastic bags and tubes and she'd laugh when she farted 'cos the stink cleared the room and I think about hitchhiking down Highway 101 at 15 and how the first man who took me to his apartment and gave me porn magazines to look at while he swallowed my cock didn't even pay me 'cos I was too scared to say you owe me. That's the first time I've said that, that I was scared. But you would never know, that's what my life has been about, making sure you can't tell what's happening inside. Burning the past is hard for a wretch like me as I'm attached to the legend of glorious filth I have constructed, a magical circle around myself, to keep you on guard and to make sure I stay 12 years old for eternity.

POSTSCRIPT

I'm putting the paint on the lining paper using brushes then sponges and then I'm in a hurry so I just use my hands and like I said I'm a little touched so as the paint starts to dry I'm seeing faces and bodies rising up out of the graveyard all over the paper. I blink my eyes but they're still there, yes, ghosts are manifesting through my hands onto the things I touch and they're trying to tell their story, their rage and their shame and their love but only certain people can see them besides me, only people who have been truly fucked and broken can make out the faces and dancing bodies spinning themselves into existence and then I take a photograph and bam, there he is, a fat Aleister Crowley in full ceremonial robes with a skull in the background is staring straight out of the print, and I'm thinking you old dog, I got ya, I got ya, I'm going to teach you how to love, Aleister, you got the hell part down pat but the missing ingredient is pure unadulterated bone-smashing love and when it comes it sails you like a wild horse over the hypnotised ocean and each time your hooves touch the waves a new scar appears on your skin that bears witness to the song that sings you into being and once you've heard that song there's no going back, because you've broken through and you're damned if you break stride for a second and the only place to go is straight into the sun and it burns you to dust and you come out the other side as the baby in Ria's belly but this time it's different because you've been kissed by the horse latitudes and nothing will ever be the same.